Frank Lloyd Wright and the Prairie School

Frank Lloyd Wright

Taliesin, Spring Green, Wisconsin,
  begun 1911; rebuilt 1914 and 1925

Courtyard

Photograph courtesy H.R. Hitchcock

Frank Lloyd Wright and the Prairie School

H. Allen Brooks

George Braziller, Inc., New York
published in association with the
Cooper-Hewitt Museum
The Smithsonian Institution's National Museum of Design

Copyright © 1984 H. Allen Brooks

Published by **George Braziller, Inc.**
One Park Avenue, New York, NY 10016

in association with the

Cooper-Hewitt Museum
2 East 91st Street, New York, NY 10128

Library of Congress Cataloging in Publication Data

Brooks, H. Allen (Harold Allen), 1925–
  Frank Lloyd Wright and the Prairie School.

  Bibliography: p.
  Includes index.
  1. Wright, Frank Lloyd, 1867–1959.   2. Prairie
School (Architecture).   I. Title.
NA737.W7B76   1983   720′.92′4   83-15621
ISBN 0-8076-1084-4 (pbk.)

Printed in the United States of America

Designed by Katy Homans, Homans/Salsgiver

Second Printing

Cover illustration

Frank Lloyd Wright

Henry J. Allen House, Wichita,
Kansas, 1917

Dining room table and chairs

Pencil and colored pencils on tracing
paper; 37 × 44.7 cm.

Cooper-Hewitt Museum:
Smithsonian Regents' Acquisitions
Fund and Friends of Drawings and
Prints

Contents

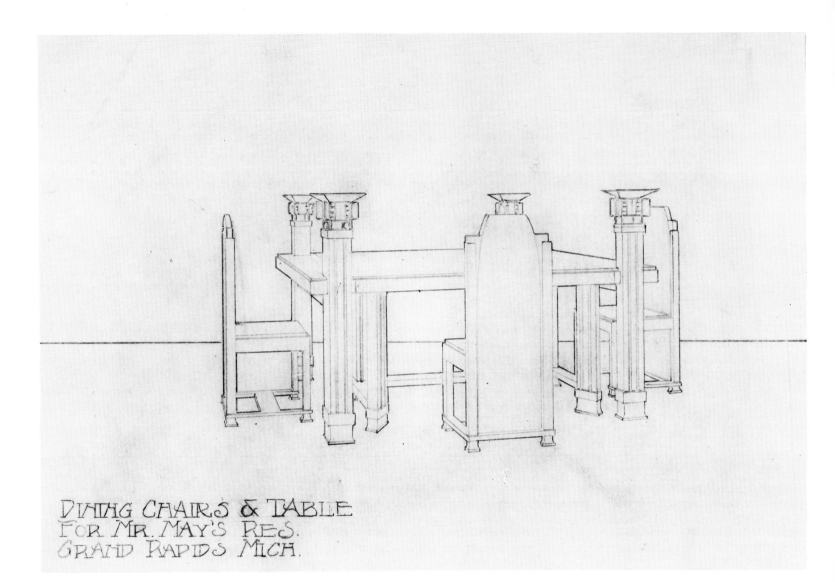

DINING CHAIRS & TABLE
FOR MR. MAY'S RES.
GRAND RAPIDS MICH.

Foreword

The current revival of interest in Frank Lloyd Wright is hardly surprising. To call this a revival is not, in fact, entirely accurate, since from the very beginning Wright's work has continued to be the focus of much critical attention, both here and abroad. Today, nearly twenty-five years after his death, the appeal of his architecture and design has never been greater.

The reasons are clear enough. During a career that spanned more than seven decades, Wright displayed a capacity for formal invention without parallel in the history of American architecture. The scope of his production was truly remarkable, ranging from immense visionary schemes, such as the project for the Mile High Skyscraper and the constantly evolving plan for Broadacre City, to his innumerable essays on the theme of the single-family house, which Wright continued to recast in new and highly original forms. In all of this can be seen Wright's insistence upon a completely unified approach to design: the intimate relation between building and site; the clear expression of materials, structure, and plan; and the total integration of furnishings and ornament within the architectural setting. This was, and continues to be, a commonly held ideal; but few realized it as completely as did Wright.

It is all too easy to see Wright as an isolated figure, well in advance of his time. While there can be no doubt as to the revolutionary character of his achievement, one cannot fully appreciate his legacy without an understanding of the context in which he matured as an artist or without some knowledge of his midwestern contemporaries, collectively known as the Prairie School, who participated with him in the creation of a new and uniquely American architecture.

What is most striking about their work is its optimism and genuine sense of purpose—a spirit which is characteristic of much of the new architecture at the turn of the century—and its earnest moral tone, perhaps best described by the dual imperative that their work be both "simple" and "honest." Theirs was a fundamentally American approach, although one based on principles that were recognized and applauded far beyond our borders.

The Cooper-Hewitt Museum was delighted when George Braziller suggested that we join in the publication of this volume, which was inspired by the museum's exhibition of the same title; many of the illustrations are drawn from objects shown in it. I would like to take this opportunity to acknowledge gratefully the many individuals and institutions who loaned works to us, as well as to thank the Friends of the Cooper-Hewitt Museum, who sponsored the exhibition, and those members of the staff who contributed to its success: Lillian H. Clagett, Elaine E. Dee, Dorothy T. Globus, Steven Langehough, David R. McFadden, Robin Parkinson, Cordelia Rose, and Timothy F. Rub, Ford Foundation Fellow at the museum, as well as Scott Elliott. Above all, we wish to thank Professor H. Allen Brooks for sharing with us his insights about Frank Lloyd Wright.

Lisa Taylor, Director
Cooper-Hewitt Museum
The Smithsonian Institution's National Museum of Design

Introduction: Frank Lloyd Wright and the Prairie School

The Prairie School, that group of architects practicing in the American Midwest from the turn of the century until about 1920, was a regional manifestation of a much larger ferment then occurring in architecture and the decorative arts. In Europe and America the modern movement began as a series of subcultures seeking alternatives to prevailing practices in design, especially to the revitalized Classical Revival that by 1900 was again the dominant mode. There was the English Arts and Crafts Movement led by William Morris; the Glasgow Four, including Charles Rennie Mackintosh; the Art Nouveau, exemplified by the architecture of Antonio Gaudí, Victor Horta, and Henry van de Velde; and the Vienna Secession, with Otto Wagner, Josef Hoffmann, Joseph Olbrich, and Adolf Loos; others were less closely associated with a particular group or style: H. P. Berlage, Auguste Perret, and Peter Behrens. In America there was the Chicago School —including such firms as Adler and Sullivan, Burnham and Root, and Holabird and Roche—which built the first truly modern skyscrapers late in the nineteenth century. They, in turn, were succeeded by the younger men and women of the Prairie School, whose principal concern was the single-family house.

The Prairie School included such notable talents as Barry Byrne, William Drummond, George Elmslie, Walter Burley Griffin, Marion Mahony, William Purcell, and Louis Sullivan, yet unlike its international counterparts it also claimed a man of genius, Frank Lloyd Wright. He and his colleagues achieved a remarkable architectural synthesis that, while honoring the immediate past, united such diverse factors as traditional values, vernacular building styles, classical ideals, and natural materials. Simultaneously, they were able to reconcile client pragmatism with high art. In formal terms, their work was characterized by a horizontal disposition of lines and masses, interspersed with a spirited interplay of shorter verticals, such as piers and other subsidiary forms, all coalesced into an organic whole that imparted a sense of repose to their designs. They were neither outmoded practitioners of the nineteenth century nor twentieth-century revolutionaries. Rather, they were basically conservative, upholding the values of their time and place and interpreting them into something contemporary in spirit and uniquely American. This was their great achievement and pinpoints the reason for their present-day appeal.

And what is American about these designs? Most important, it is their theoretical connection with nature, the design process being derived from natural laws rather than philosophical idealism or classical rules. One must go to the school of nature, Louis Sullivan insisted, and this is precisely what Wright and other Prairie School architects did. Wright, whose understanding of this principle was the most profound, later referred to it as "organic architecture." Like nature, design should adapt perfectly to function, thus insuring a definite beauty. The creative process was "organic," unfolding or growing from the inside out, establishing integral relationships between plan and elevation, interior space and external expression, architecture and decoration.

Equally American was the emphasis these architects placed upon a close relation between building and landscape, permitting the house to blend comfortably into its setting whether it be the flat horizontal prairie, a hillside (color pl. 5), or even a dramatic cliff (pl. 63). Their use of natural materials, especially ones found in the Midwest (pine, oak, limestone), the practice of leaving the exterior woodwork unplaned, unpainted but stained, as well as their preference for staining and waxing the interior woodwork to reveal the texture and grain also contributed to the building's intimate relation to its setting. The innate characteristics of the materials became a principal medium of expression, and even ornament—art glass, friezes, architectural sculpture—was based upon stylized, regional flora, further contributing to the regionalism of these designs.

American, too, was the openness of both the interior and exterior of these houses. Rooms unfolded, interpenetrated, merged, and became fewer in number but more diversified and flexible in function. Emphasis was placed upon use and convenience, and this resulted in an amazing lucidity and logic in the plan. Exteriors often became more transparent, perme-

able, and open, with the sharp cantilevers and broadly overhanging roofs creating voids and hollows.

The regional identity of this architecture was also evidenced by its assimilation of vernacular building types; in particular, the ubiquitous, low-cost, foursquare house so central to the theme of Sinclair Lewis's novel *Main Street*, itself set in the Midwest just prior to the First World War. This form (fig. 7) was reworked repeatedly by the prairie architects (pls. 59–66), as was the popular L- or T-plan, with a doorway at the angle and with a shelf roof, usually over a veranda, running along one side (pl. 11).

Finally, and less immediately evident, was the uniquely American acceptance of the machine as a natural and essential complement to the architectural process. The mechanical saw, press, or mold were able to produce boards, bricks, or terracotta and concrete blocks of distinctive character; steel beams and reinforced concrete made possible the far-reaching, cantilevered roofs and balconies. Unlike the Englishman William Morris, who had rejected the machine as an enemy of art, or the International Style designers, who would make a virtual fetish of standardized, industrial parts and place a symbolic value on the relationship between the machine and art, the Prairie School architects, led by Wright, accepted the machine as part of their natural heritage and used it to shape, but not to dominate, their aesthetic. Therefore, their buildings benefited from modern technology but still retained their natural, regional, and distinctly American style.

The Prairie School could not have existed without a certain concurrence of objectives and ideals between the architects and their clients. This sharing of values helps explain why the movement occurred where and when it did. Especially important were such factors as the Arts and Crafts Movement, the vogue for bungalows, and the encouragement offered these architects by homemaker magazines, an entirely new type of publication that made its appearance in Chicago in 1896 with the founding of *House Beautiful*—the first magazine ever to write about Wright's work.

The Arts and Crafts Movement pleaded for reform in the visual arts by embracing such things as simplicity, respect for materials, and handicraft; its message was directed both at artists and the public. It began in England in the nineteenth century with William Morris as founder and chief protagonist, and it took the form of a reaction against the values of the Victorian era. Chicago became one of the earliest and most important centers of arts and crafts activities in North America, but this occurred only after Morris's death in 1896. The local movement got under way at Hull House, Jane Addams's renowned settlement house, where the Chicago Arts and Crafts Society was founded in 1897. Frank Lloyd Wright, Robert Spencer, Irving and Allen Pond, Dwight Perkins, and Myron Hunt—all early Prairie School participants—were among the charter members. It was also at Hull House, in 1901, that Wright read his manifesto, "The Art and Craft of the Machine," in which he lauded Morris yet dissociated Morris's abhorrence of machine production from his message of elimination and truth to materials. In stunning contrast to Morris, Wright argued that the machine, if correctly used, was precisely the means by which these goals could be achieved. He noted, for example, that the power-driven saw "teaches us that the beauty of wood lies first in its qualities as wood . . . a material having . . . intrinsic artistic properties, of which its beautiful markings is one, its texture another, its color a third."[1]

Related to the Arts and Crafts Movement was the popular enthusiasm for unpretentious bungalows, which were rustic and appealed to the practical "do-it-yourself" sensibility of the time. Indeed, the prairie house, with its low, spreading forms, was regarded by many as a midwestern version of the bungalow. Likewise, Gustav Stickley's Craftsman homes, vauntingly displayed in his arts-and-crafts-oriented *Craftsman* magazine (founded in 1901) were, notwithstanding their crude plans and utter lack of artistic sensitivity, also a vehicle for distracting attention from prevalent historical styles—especially the "classical" or closely related "colonial," which reigned nearly supreme after the Chicago World's Fair of 1893.

Yet the real mentors of middle-class

household taste were the homemaker magazines. Ladies' magazines, like *Godey's Lady's Book* or *Ladies' Home Journal*, had long existed, but these catered to the upper-class lady rather than the active, more liberated middle-class woman who no longer was restricted to embroidery but was free to work in the garden or to dirty her hands at the potter's wheel. For her, the arts and crafts held the appeal of participation, of self-involvement, and *House Beautiful* was the champion of this cause. Eventually, of course, there was competition in the field: *House and Garden* was founded in 1901, *American Homes and Gardens* in 1905, and *Better Homes and Gardens* in 1922; yet it was *House Beautiful* that published designs by Prairie School architects more consistently than any other journal.

Wright's clients, as confirmed in surveys by Leonard Eaton and Eugene Streich,[2] were mostly upper-middle-class families in which the husband was a businessman (often an executive) with certain technical or engineering skills, or perhaps a member of the professions with a higher than average level of education. One or both spouses might have a strong interest in music or theater, and apparently they were more independent-minded than the average person. These were people who made their own decisions, for whom intuition was more valid than imported culture. Wright said of his clients that they were "American men of business with unspoiled instincts and ideals. A man of this type usually has the faculty of judging for him-

self. He has rather liked the 'idea' . . . because the 'common sense' of the thing appeals to him."[3] In short, Midwesterners still enjoyed the freedom of frontier pragmatism, or matter-of-factness, that allowed them to shun certain cultural constraints. Writings by and about Midwesterners confirm this spirit, and even place names bear out this attitude: Oak Park, River Forest, Spring Green, Mason City—towns where the prairie architects worked—are names not inherited from another time or place. This freedom was lost after 1914; by then, however, it existed in southern California, where for more than a decade Wright, R. M. Schindler, the Greene brothers, Irving Gill, Richard J. Neutra, and others found clients who appreciated "the 'common sense' of the thing" without deference to other cultures' values.

These are some of the reasons why the Prairie School could exist and why its homeland was the American Midwest. It was the absence, or withdrawal, of these conditions, and the introduction of new cultural values and fashions, that led, after the First World War, to its untimely end.

Also important for an understanding of the Prairie School is a knowledge of the background and training of several of the architects, the formation of the group, and the relations which evolved between these designers, particularly with regard to Wright.

Frank Lloyd Wright (1867–1959) was born in Wisconsin. He spent most teenage summers on an uncle's farm where he garnered his lifelong respect for nature's materials and the process of organic growth. Despite his mother's decision, even before his birth, that her son would become an architect, Wright, like many architects of his generation, never attended architectural school. Instead one of his earliest contacts with building was when the Chicago architect Joseph Lyman Silsbee constructed a small Unitarian chapel on his uncles' farmlands near Spring Green, Wisconsin, in 1886 (fig. 1). This superb design, beside which Wright lies buried, introduced Wright to the Shingle Style with its textured, wraparound, shingled cladding and minimal variations in materials, as well as its sense of order and natural repose.[4] Three years later, when designing his own home in Oak Park, Illinois, this was the style Wright would adopt (pl. 1).[5]

Upon moving to Chicago in 1887 Wright gained employment first with Silsbee and shortly thereafter with the firm of Adler and Sullivan, with which he remained six years. Hired to draw ornament (pl. 4), he was soon given the opportunity to design the various houses that the partners felt obliged to undertake in addition to their tall commercial buildings. Wright learned much from Louis Sullivan (1856–1924), yet Sullivan's most important lesson was to lead Wright back to nature, instilling in him the concept that all design—whether ornament or architecture—was founded upon natural laws.

After leaving Sullivan in 1893 his first commission was the William Winslow House in River Forest, where the 26-year-old Wright created a masterpiece that had the nobility, presence, and balanced proportions of classicism, without using the forms and decorative details of classical design (pl. 6).[6] But rather than capitalize upon this success, Wright undertook a period of experimentation and research that for several years led to inconsistencies and irregular quality in his work. Then, finally, he achieved the long-sought prototype for a prairie house in a project for the *Ladies' Home Journal* in 1900–1901 (pl. 11).

This breakthrough came about while Wright was actively involved with other architects who like himself had come under the influence of Louis Sullivan. For most of them, Sullivan became the philosophical leader around whose banner they rallied late in the 1890s. Vocal, spirited, and united by common goals, they gathered at Steinway Hall (where they shared office space on the topmost floor), formed a short-lived luncheon club called "The Eighteen," and briefly dominated the executive positions of the local draftsmen's organization, the Chicago Architectural Club, which in turn helped establish the Architectural League of America in 1899. "Inspiring days they were, I am sure, for us all," Wright declared.[7]

Rhetoric, however, failed to translate into architectural designs—with the result that no clear direction was discernible in their work. Sullivan continued to provide spiritual inspiration,[8] yet was unable to direct the younger architects in their search for appropriate and innovative residential designs. It remained for the more gifted Wright to create an architectural language that would express Sullivan's ideas of natural laws and simultaneously provide a clear and viable direction in design. This synthesis was evident for all to see when the Chicago Architectural Club exhibition opened at the Art Institute in the spring of 1902. The entire group was represented; a separate section within the galleries (and in the profusely illustrated catalogue which contained a frontispiece specially designed by Sullivan) was devoted to Wright's work—drawings, plans, photographs, architectural models, art glass, furnishings, vases, flower arrangements—totalling sixty-five exhibits in all. In short, the exhibition provided a clear "statement of position" for each architect and manifestly established Wright as the leader of the group. All, however, were not sympathetic to his innovative ideas, and this caused a certain realignment as several of the earlier, often older, adherents, including George Dean, Hugh Garden, Myron Hunt, Dwight Perkins, Irving and Allen Pond, Richard Schmidt, and Webster Tomlinson, after brief flirtations with Wright's ideas, went their more independent ways.

With each loss, however, there was an eventual gain as other, usually younger, architects joined the cause. Barry Byrne (1883–1967), impressed by Wright's exhibit but without prior experience, applied for an apprenticeship at Wright's Oak Park Studio in 1902. A number of architects who were to be important contributors to the Prairie School were already working there: Marion Mahony (1871–1962), who held a degree in architecture from the Massachusetts Institute of Technology, had begun her periodic employment with Wright in 1896; William Drummond (1876–1946), who initially joined Wright in 1899; and Walter Burley Griffin (1876–1937), who, after graduating in architecture from the University of Illinois in 1899 and briefly working at Steinway Hall, moved to the Studio in 1901. Subsequent years saw others such as Albert McArthur, Harry Robinson, Charles E. White, Jr., Andrew Willatzen, and Francis C. Sullivan added to the Studio's ranks. Louis Sullivan's office continued to provide instruction for future Prairie School designers—including, in addition to Wright, George Elmslie (1871–1952), Parker Berry, William Steele, and, briefly, William Gray Purcell (1880–1965). Meanwhile, John Van Bergen (1885–1969) took his initial training under Griffin.[9]

Once these younger men added their strength to those already practicing, including Robert C. Spencer, Jr. (1865–1953), Thomas E. Tallmadge (1876–1940), and his future partner Vernon S. Watson (1878–1950), the movement was on very solid footing. Sullivan augmented the group's production beginning in 1906 with his first prairie-style design, the bank at Owatonna, Minnesota (pls. 69, 70), and with the Henry Babson House in Riverside of the following year (pls. 35, 36). 1906 saw Griffin enter private practice and in 1907 Purcell and George Feick founded their Minneapolis firm, joined two years later by Elmslie, who left Sullivan's employ after twenty years' loyal service. Drummond began working on his own in 1909, the same year that Willatzen and Byrne created a partnership in Seattle (but in 1914 Byrne returned to the Midwest to take over Griffin's office after the latter left for Australia). Thus by 1909 the make-up of the group had greatly changed, the effect being to enhance Wright's pre-eminence. His influence increased not only because several younger architects had apprenticed at his Studio but because in the interval Wright had produced a truly remarkable body of important work.

Wright's Studio was a dynamic center of activity during the first decade of the twentieth century. He preferred to work, with his staff, at home: first in the Studio, which he added to his Oak Park home in 1898 (pl. 8) and, after 1911, at Taliesin, where in 1932 he established the Taliesin Fellowship for the training of young architects (frontispiece, color pl. 5, pls. 47, 48). He also maintained a downtown office, as at Steinway Hall, where he met clients rather than worked. The Oak Park Studio consisted of a reception area, a little octagonal library (pl. 7), an office, and a small two-story drafting room (see plan, pl. 8) where the environment was congenial and informal. Some of Wright's six

children might play on the balcony above the drafting room, or the sculptor Richard Bock might use it as a place to work. Depending on the pressure of work, there were four to six architects plus Wright's secretary and bookkeeper, Isabel Roberts, on the staff. More than a dozen had apprenticed there by 1909, but the attrition rate was rather high, due partly to Wright's callousness concerning pay. Griffin, before his departure late in 1905, was office manager, job superintendent, and the person with whom Wright most liked to discuss his current work. As their skills developed, Drummond and Byrne increasingly took charge of specific projects, including drafting and the supervision of construction. Mahony continued her periodic employ. John Van Bergen, fresh from Griffin's office, was the last to join (January 1909) and, with Isabel Roberts, the last to leave. There were also others who stayed shorter lengths of time.

The Studio was no place for individual expression since Wright maintained strict control over all designs. Yet personalities (or "hands") did emerge in the beautiful perspective renderings, although Wright established the formula and monitored the results. His interest in Japanese prints, of which he was a great connoisseur and collector, was important in determining the Studio style: on the lovely de Rhodes House (1906) drawing, where Marion Mahony's monogram, MLM, appears, he astutely wrote, "Drawn by Mahony— After FLlW and Hiroshige." Wright's avid interest in photography also played a role, though not one that he was likely to admit. My research has shown that most of these eye-level views of buildings, once thought of as presentation drawings, were actually traced on a light box from photographs of the finished structures.[10] Such tracings resulted in correct perspective and at the same time created an outline of flat surfaces that recalled Japanese prints. The Ward Willits House and Susan Dana House drawings (pls. 12, 14) are among those traced. Another influence on the Studio drawings was probably the rendering technique of Harvey Ellis, the celebrated midwestern delineator whose late-nineteenth-century designs, uniting a linear style with massive foliage, bear a striking resemblance to Wright's drawings. Since many buildings, and even their surrounding trees, were traced from photographs, the latitude for individual expression was pretty much limited to foliage and flowering plants. In this realm Mahony's hand is the most distinctive (pls. 29, 59), though one can more hesitatingly identify the work of Wright (pls. 2, 8), Drummond (pl. 11), Birch Burdette Long, and later, Emil Brodelle (pl. 80).

One hundred of the Studio drawings, plans, and details were published by Ernst Wasmuth of Berlin, Germany, in a boxed, two-volume folio. This was the first monograph ever devoted to Wright's work. Printed by direct lithography using brown, white, gold, and other tones on various types of paper, these memoirs of the Studio were published as *Ausgeführte Bauten und Entwürfe von Frank Lloyd Wright* in 1910. For this project Wright and his staff retraced existing drawings, created new ones, and modified certain others. Their work began at the Studio and was completed at Fiesole, Italy, where Wright moved temporarily, having abandoned his wife, family, and clients and closed the Studio in the autumn of 1909.

The influence of these drawings was strongly felt among Wright's associates in the American Midwest. Some, like Percy Dwight Bentley, imitated Mahony's style; others, like Purcell and Elmslie (pls. 50, 56) or Byrne (pl. 66), tried variations of their own. Certain drawings pose attribution problems, such as the Dexter Ferry Project (pl. 52) designed by Drummond, who was a skilled renderer (see pl. 64), yet the foliage is not executed in his manner. Rather it is in Mahony's style and was probably drawn by her. Her technique vacillated between a preference for tight, closed forms (pl. 29) and more lyrical, active outlines (pls. 63, 89), although in some instances she mixed the two together.

The publication of the Wasmuth folios and the concurrent exhibit in Berlin of the original drawings (pls. 8, 11, 12, 14, 29, 51, 59) was an event that modified the course of architecture in central Europe, as evidenced by the architectural journals of subsequent years. Architects like Mies van der Rohe and Walter Gropius, both then working for Peter Behrens, got their first close look at Wright's work. Mies later recalled (and he might well have been speaking for the midwestern architects eight years earlier when they saw Wright's work at the Chicago Architectural Club exhibit in 1902):

> We young architects found ourselves in painful inner conflict. We were ready to pledge ourselves to an idea. But the potential vitality of the architectural idea of this period had, by this time, been lost.
>
> This, then, was the situation in 1910.
>
> At this moment, so critical for us, there came to Berlin the exhibition of the work of Frank Lloyd Wright. . . .
>
> The work of this great master revealed an architectural world of unexpected force and clarity of language, and also a disconcerting richness of form. Here finally was a master-builder drawing upon the veritable fountainhead of architecture, who with true originality lifted his architectural creations into the light. Here, again, at last, genuine organic architecture flowered.
>
> . . . The dynamic impulse emanating from his work invigorated a whole generation. His influence was strongly felt even when it was not actually visible.[11]

In 1911 Wasmuth again published Wright's buildings, this time in a less expensive, more readily available book of photographs. That same year the Dutch architect H. P. Berlage visited America on an itinerary largely planned by William Purcell; after the tour Berlage lectured throughout central Europe on Sullivan and Wright. Before the decade was out Wright's work was appearing regularly in the avant-garde periodicals of Holland, and ultimately had a profound influence on both the Amsterdam School and the de Stijl group. By these means Europe knew of the Prairie School, but almost exclusively through the work of Wright in spite of the fact that his colleagues' designs occasionally appeared in various European journals.

Walter Burley Griffin also enjoyed considerable overseas success, but ultimately his influence was limited mostly to Australia and India, where Wright's work was little known. In 1911 he had entered the international competition for the plan of Canberra, the new city that would become the capital of Australia. Marion Mahony rendered the plans and drawings; he won the competition, and she won Griffin in marriage. Thereafter her drawing skill was devoted to his cause, and soon her technique attained its greatest perfection. India ink on linen (without shading) was her favored medium, and this published extremely well (pls. 46, 63, 89). Often she transferred the drawing onto silk or satin and tinted it with watercolor. This resulted in a softer effect, almost like a Chinese painting, but in black and white it reproduced less well (fig. 9). The colored prints were intended for exhibitions, the most important of which opened at the Musée des Arts Décoratifs in Paris in 1914

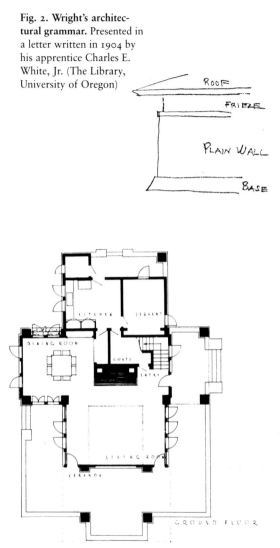

Fig. 2. Wright's architectural grammar. Presented in a letter written in 1904 by his apprentice Charles E. White, Jr. (The Library, University of Oregon)

ROOF
FRIEZE
PLAIN WALL
BASE

Fig. 3. Frank Lloyd Wright. Charles S. Ross House, Delavan Lake, Wisconsin, 1902. Plan (Hitchcock, *In the Nature of Materials*)

before continuing on to Vienna. There, however, the tour was cut short, failing to open because of the outbreak of war. One wonders what influence these splendid renderings, and Griffin's architecture, would have had if the tour had been able to continue.

We have spoken of Wright's project for the *Ladies' Home Journal* (pl. 11) as a prototype for the prairie house. Shortly thereafter, he refined this concept in a series of executed designs beginning with two houses at Kankakee, followed by the Frank Thomas House at Oak Park (which was still transitional because it was awkwardly positioned too high off the ground; color pl. 1), and finally the Willits House of 1901–2 at Highland Park (pl. 12), where Wright achieved a complete synthesis of the components of the prairie style (fig. 2). However, maturity did not mean a rigid or static formula; the designs for his prairie houses continually evolved as evidenced by the relative ease with which almost any design can be dated on the basis of its forms.

For the long-term future of architecture (speaking of generations or even centuries hence) Wright's major innovation was to design interior spaces that were not enclosed in the traditional sense. This revolutionary concept was one of the greatest contributions ever made to architecture. Once explained, it looks deceptively simple yet it would be difficult to overestimate the magnitude of Wright's achievement.

Prior to Wright, public spaces in domestic architecture had single, clearly defined uses: living room, dining room, vestibule, or den. Each room was a box bound by its corners and enclosed by its four walls. Use was largely determined by the furnishings. By modifying the system of enclosure, Wright created space that was relative to the changing position and needs of the user. This had both practical and psychological benefits: practical because the building seemed larger than it actually was (clients got more for their money); psychological because of a sense of relaxation accrued from believing the interior was more open and expansive than it was. Furthermore, the various visual perspectives introduced by Wright reduced the tensions of monotonous or claustrophobic rooms.

Wright achieved this "destruction of the box" simultaneously with his prototype for the prairie house of 1900–1901. This is evident in the Willits and Charles Ross Houses (pl. 12, fig. 3), where the living and dining rooms interpenetrate and overlap at their corners. He thereby created a diagonal, yet restricted, view between these "rooms" (fig. 4). Soon he would obliterate all corners. The wall, which no longer served to connect the corners, became more like a screen, a slab, or a plane that delimited a space rather than actually enclosing it. Thus, a space could have more than a single function. Its purpose could change in accordance with the activity or position of the observer. In the plan of the Darwin D. Martin House (pl. 19) we see how Wright employed short screens and piers to define the still some-

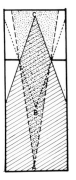

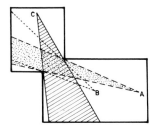

Fig. 4. **Shingle Style versus Frank Lloyd Wright.** Above: typical Shingle Style plan with generous openings between the principal rooms. Below: in a Wright house one room may penetrate into another at the corner. Note, however, that Wright achieves greater privacy from all positions: A, B, or C (Drawings by H. A. Brooks)

what traditional rooms; note too how the rhythm of these piers and screens is expressed on the exterior (pl. 17). Later, and especially in his Usonian houses, such screens would be more freely and inventively arranged.[12]

Of the other prairie architects, only a few used Wright's spatial devices (except when designing foursquare houses). Several, however, developed solutions sufficiently personal so that the designer's identity is revealed by a study of the plan. Griffin, conditions permitting, contravened tradition by setting rooms at half-levels to each other in a vertical tier. He did this at the William H. Emery House of 1901 (pl. 13) as well as at the larger of two houses designed for Hurd Comstock (pl. 46). By contrast, Marion Mahony preferred a single horizontal axis along which each room ran either lengthwise or crosswise—like a well-loaded skewer. Purcell and Elmslie showed the greatest variety in their planning and often a considerable indebtedness to Wright. Their Decker House plan (pl. 50) is derived from Wright's "A Home in a Prairie Town" (a project designed for the *Ladies' Home Journal*) and its various progeny such as the Martin House plan (pl. 19). Yet Purcell's own Minneapolis home displays a highly original spatial plan that completely denies the modest size of the house (pls. 54–57). The on-line living and dining rooms share a common, tentlike ceiling that expands the visual space of one room over that of the other. But their floor levels are not the same; the dining room (the function of which is more intimate) has a seemingly lower ceiling because of the higher floor, which, with its low parapet, allows for a visual separation between these two rooms. Close to this parapet, tucked in the corner, is a writing nook with furnishings and glass designed by Elmslie (pl. 57).

Wright had confronted a similar spatial problem when designing the dining and living rooms at the Frederick Robie House (fig. 5, pls. 37–39). His solution was completely different and characteristically Wrightian. He inverted tradition. Instead of opening up the intervening wall at its center, and leaving rudimentary spurs clinging to the corners, he abolished the corners and placed a fireplace at the center. This permitted an uninterrupted flow of space along both sides of the fireplace and along a lengthy range of French doors which, depending on the location of the beholder, became part of either the living room or the dining room. Wright heightened this sense of spatial continuity by allowing the ceiling to pass through the upper part of the chimney mass and to continue into the adjoining room, and by adding wooden strips to the ceiling to echo the rhythm of doors and windows.

The interior of the Robie House, particularly its dining room (pl. 39), is among Wright's best-known works and exemplifies the perfect unity he obtained between the various arts. The theme of horizontals versus verticals remains consistent throughout. The built-in sideboard, with its architectonic forms, picks up the

Fig. 5. Frank Lloyd Wright.
Frederick C. Robie House,
Chicago, Illinois, 1908–9,
Living Room (Photograph:
Chicago Architectural Pho-
tographing Co.)

rhythms of the architecture, as does the table with its piers and cantilevered slabs. The formal slat-back chairs, like movable screens, define the area for dining, while their emphatically rectilinear backs restate notes that are sounded throughout the house. The window glass (pl. 42), light fixtures, and rug are also by the architect. Compare, stylistically, the equally complete ensemble by Elmslie for the writing nook at the Edna S. Purcell House (pl. 57).

Whenever possible the prairie architects designed everything within a house in order to ensure a perfect artistic harmony. No commercial furniture was entirely satisfactory, although when economy was required Mission or Craftsman pieces were sometimes used. However, these were thicker, heavier, and cruder than the highly sophisticated designs by Wright, Elmslie, or George Niedecken, and introduced a disturbing note into the interiors. Traditional furniture was completely out of place. Nor was Wright willing to create a series of standard types: with but rare exceptions, each set of furniture was unique to the building for which it was designed. Even in the era of the Arts and Crafts Movement, when handicraft skills were relatively common, this proved a tremendous undertaking. George M. Niedecken (1878–1945), founder of the Niedecken-Walbridge Company of "interior architects" in Milwaukee, was therefore a godsend for Wright and other prairie architects who used his services (including Purcell and Elmslie, Tallmadge and Watson, Spencer and Powers, Drummond, Bentley, and von Holst). Wright first knew Niedecken as an artist, having employed him to paint the naturalistic frieze around the Dana House dining room (color pl. 2; compare this with Wright's conventionalized sumac design for the Dana House windows, pl. 15). Usually Wright provided Niedecken with a sketch (pl. 83), or perhaps a scale drawing (color pl. 7). After detailing it Niedecken would obtain approval from the architect and then see to its manufacture and installation. In the Robie House, for example, the furniture was built by the F. H. Bresler Company of Milwaukee, the windows were by the Linden Glass Company of Chicago (which also did the Dana House and Avery Coonley House glass), while the carpets were woven in Austria.[13] Niedecken supervised the completion of the interiors. In fact, he made his own proposal for the living room which Wright did not accept (pl. 40; note how the wall and window treatment differs from that

which was executed, fig. 5). However, other architects and clients often gave Niedecken a freer hand in design than Wright allowed.

Sculptors were also sought for collaboration, notably Richard Bock (1865–1949), who worked at the Dana House and Larkin Company Administration Building (pls. 23, 24), and Alfonso Iannelli (1888–1965), who was the major contributor at Midway Gardens (pls. 76–78). Iannelli also executed the architectural sculpture for Purcell and Elmslie at the Woodbury County Courthouse in Sioux City, Iowa (pl. 75), and assisted Byrne on various ecclesiastical commissions.

The stylistic unity that embraced all the furnishings and architecture for a single commission also had broader implications for the architect's oeuvre, with one design element often holding the key to a variety of possibilities. For example, we can see the potential for a building plan in the pattern of Wright's rug design for the Bogk House of 1916 (pl. 79). We also find the light standards and needles of Midway Gardens (pl. 77), or possibly the elements of a table (pl. 86), floor lamp (color pl. 7), or umbrella stand (pl. 85). Then, too, there is a motif almost resembling the hollyhock used on the Aline Barnsdall House and its dining room chairs (pls. 87, 88). This interdisciplinary use of motifs demonstrates how the decorative arts and architecture were truly indivisible.

More than any other Prairie School architect, Wright was fortunate in having various well-to-do patrons who could

Fig. 6. Mid-nineteenth-century bracketed house. La Crosse, Wisconsin (Photograph: H. A. Brooks)

Fig. 7. Early twentieth-century foursquare house. Between Houston and Rushford, Minnesota (Photograph: H. A. Brooks)

afford these custom furnishings. Yet this creates the illusion, fostered by the propensity of his more expensive homes to attract attention and to become house-museums, that these were typical commissions. Nothing could be further from the truth; they were the exceptions and not the rule. Prairie School architects built for the middle class and Wright for one made a concerted effort to devise agreeable low-cost housing. Early examples were his project "A Fireproof House for $5,000" published in the *Ladies' Home Journal* of April 1907 and his carefully designed partial prefabs called "American System Ready-Cut" for the Richard Brothers of Milwaukee in 1915. And, beginning in 1937, he would develop the Usonian house, a type which, though small and economical, combined all the spatial advantages of his prairie houses.

"A Fireproof House for $5,000" (fireproof because of its intended concrete construction) was notable in several respects (pl. 59). It was based on the popular foursquare vernacular type and its cubic shapes made it inexpensive and efficient to construct and to heat. Figure 6 illustrates a mid-nineteenth-century example of the foursquare house and figure 7 is an example dating from the early twentieth century; compare figure 7 with George Maher's John Farson House (fig. 13) or Wright's William H. Winslow House (pl. 6). In the Fireproof House Wright ordered the apertures and gave emphasis to the corners. Even in this small building, he

managed to combine interior openness with visual privacy by using a fireplace to divide the two principal rooms, while at the same time uniting them visually with a common band of windows (an arrangement he repeated at the Robie House; pls. 38, 59). Wright built several houses of this type (with lath and plaster, never with concrete) which became his single most influential design for the other architects of the Prairie School. Most devised variations on the theme by borrowing not only from Wright's plan and motif but also from the vernacular. The secret, however, was to attain harmonious proportions, and curiously enough it was often the least inventive architects who produced the most successful schemes. The Edward C. Bartl House by Percy Dwight Bentley (1885–1968) at La Crosse, Wisconsin, is a case in point, though it owes less to Wright than it does to Griffin; yet Griffin lacked Bentley's finer feeling for proportions (pl. 62). John Van Bergen, whose work generally followed Wright's quite closely, also built several foursquare houses in and around Oak Park. Other thematic variations include houses by Drummond, Griffin, Byrne, and Wright's son John (pls. 59–66).

After his 1909–10 sojourn in Europe, Wright built Taliesin (Welsh for "Shining Brow") on the farmlands of his youth near Spring Green, Wisconsin. This would be his principal home for the remainder of his life (frontispiece, color pl. 5, pls. 47, 48). His work continually evolved toward an

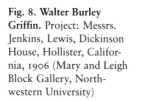

Fig. 8. Walter Burley Griffin. Project: Messrs. Jenkins, Lewis, Dickinson House, Hollister, California, 1906 (Mary and Leigh Block Gallery, Northwestern University)

increasing emphasis on abstract forms, cantilevered planes, and geometric masses. A chronological survey of his houses confirms this stylistic development: the little Mrs. Thomas H. Gale House of 1909 (pl. 51) clearly postdates the Robie design, just as both these projects date from long after the Willits and Martin Houses (compare pls. 12, 17, and 37). Similarly, the Coonley Playhouse of 1912 (pl. 53) and Midway Gardens of 1914 (pls. 76, 77) must follow the Gale design. Wright's favored cruciform plan with pyramidal massing, used at the Willits House or Coonley Playhouse, was still being employed in the first of his Californian houses, the Aline Barnsdall House (called the "Hollyhock" House) of 1917–20 (pl. 88). The "Hollyhock" House marks the transition between Wright's prairie houses, to which this design still refers, and his later work in California.

After 1909 the other Prairie School architects overshadowed Wright; they obtained most of the commissions and their designs received most of the publicity. The quality of their work was never higher. Some had to assimilate Wright's overpowering influence before they could make a contribution of their own. Others, from outside the Chicago area, who received their inspiration from publications but without benefiting from apprenticeships, now allied themselves with the Prairie School. However, they usually proved less dedicated, accepting the Prairie School's popular forms without concern for the principles that lay behind them.

During the years from 1909 to 1914 the Prairie School enjoyed its greatest success. Individual architects developed rich variations in the characteristics of their designs. These ranged from a preference for thin, crisp walls and gabled roofs to an emphasis on solidity and mass. Drummond consistently opted for the former (pls. 52, 60), while both Griffin (fig. 8, pls. 13, 63, 89) and Byrne valued the latter; Byrne insisted that it was the simplifying tendencies of Sullivan, as well as Irving

Fig. 9. Walter Burley Griffin. Rock Crest–Rock Glen, Mason City, Iowa, 1912. Rendering by Marion Mahony Griffin (Burnham Library, Art Institute of Chicago)

Gill, whom he had known in California, that inspired him most (pls. 66, 67). Sullivan preferred heavy, closed, earth-bound masses (pl. 35), a stylistic choice that helps explain his success in designing banks. He thought of banks as ornamented strongboxes, small yet monumental and imbued with a static equilibrium (pls. 69, 70, 73, 74). Purcell and Elmslie sometimes followed this approach (fig. 15), although their finest bank, at Winona (pl. 72), depends for its design upon a post and lintel motif in combination with a wall of suspended, ornamented glass. Except for Wright, no Prairie School architect could compete with the quality and variety of their work, which is attested to in the Winona bank, the Purcell House, and the Woodbury County Courthouse (pls. 72, 54–57, 75).

Judging by the number of his clients, Griffin was one of the more popular prairie architects. He extricated himself from Wright's immediate influence about 1911–12 and thereafter created a series of designs in which weighty forms of rather thick proportions usually prevailed (pls. 63, 89). He was equally interested in town planning and landscape design and often signed his name "architect and landscape

24

Fig. 10. Marion Mahony Griffin. Project: Henry Ford House, Dearborn, Michigan, 1912 (Mary and Leigh Block Gallery, Northwestern University)

Fig. 11. Spencer and Powers. Edward W. McCready House, Oak Park, Illinois, 1907. Detail of entrance (*Brickbuilder*, 1914)

architect." He designed numerous subdivisions before he left for Australia, yet only one, at Mason City, Iowa, called "Rock Crest–Rock Glen," materialized. The basic concept was to have the perimeter homeowners hold the central grounds in common, and this successful scheme is still in use (fig. 9).

Marion Mahony designed houses between 1909 and 1912 for Hermann von Holst, to whom Wright had delegated his practice when he left for Europe. She sometimes used tight, rather narrow pier forms to enliven the surface of a building; but frequently these were disquieting in their proportions, although the Ford House can be cited as an exception (fig. 10). Robert Spencer, on the other hand, liked broad, smooth wall surfaces—which stressed enclosure rather than massiveness—clearly articulated by windows. Rarely was there any spatial interpenetration in his work (fig. 11, pl. 31). He also was a journalist and wrote much in support of the Prairie School, yet his own

designs usually favored English precedents. Tallmadge and Watson (Watson being the designer in this firm) preferred rough-cast plaster accented with dark wooden strips, especially under the gables, along with a rhythm of vertical piers or pilasters to articulate the facade (fig. 12). Their houses are distinctive and easily recognizable, though some are close in style to George Maher's architecture.

George W. Maher (1864–1926) was somewhat of an outsider, but he is frequently associated with the Prairie School because of his persistent search for an American style. He did create a series of new designs, for which he deserves much credit, yet these never evolved into a viable, living style. Rather they lent themselves to duplication and repetitive usage. Thus, one speaks of the "Farson House type" (fig. 13), the "Erwin House type," or the "Schultz House type" (fig. 14). These designs enjoyed tremendous popularity and were much emulated by other architects. His influence, therefore, was pro-

Fig. 13. George W. Maher. John Farson House, Oak Park, Illinois, 1897 (Photograph: H. A. Brooks Collection)

Fig. 12. Tallmadge and Watson. H. H. Rockwell House, Oak Park, Illinois, 1910 (Photograph: H. A. Brooks Collection)

found, though never as salutory as that of Wright.

The perimeters of the Prairie School were steadily spreading outward. Converts were appearing in unexpected places: Bruce Goff in Oklahoma, R. M. Schindler and Wright's sons John and Lloyd in California, Trost and Trost in Texas, Antonin Nechodoma in Puerto Rico, Henry Klutho in Florida, Francis C. Sullivan in Ontario. Yet in suburban Chicago, the original center of activity, new commissions were very hard to find. Clients were experiencing a change of taste: they now wanted so-called Tudor or "colonial" homes. *House Beautiful* illustrated its last prairie house in 1914. Stickley's *Craftsman* magazine ceased publication in 1916; by that date the Arts and Crafts Movement, too, was definitely out of fashion. Mission Style furniture was a thing of the past. This change of taste spread more slowly into the provinces, just as those regions had accepted the Prairie School at a more tardy date. Each year prior to 1914 the Prairie School had been gaining strength. Thereafter house commissions fell off sharply, though patronage for banks and other institutional buildings was slower to recede.

Without clients, one cannot build. After 1914 the Prairie School architects had little

Fig. 14. George W. Maher.
Henry W. Schultz House,
Winnetka, Illinois, 1907
(*Western Architect*, 1909)

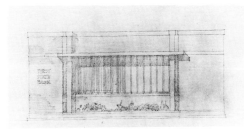

Fig. 15. Purcell and Elmslie.
First State Bank, Le Roy,
Minnesota, 1914. Archi-
tects' early rendering
(Northwest Architectural
Archives, University of
Minnesota Libraries, Min-
neapolis)

work. Their options were far from satisfactory, ranging from Purcell's early retire-
ment to Maher's apparent suicide. Sullivan
died a pauper in 1924. Wright was sustained for a while by work in Japan and
California, but eventually succumbed to
bankruptcy, the seizure of Taliesin by his
creditors, and a disastrous forced sale of
his works of art. Elmslie survived on
almost nothing, landing the rare non-
domestic commission. Byrne was fortunate
in obtaining work from the Catholic
church. Others, like Drummond and
Bentley, submitted to social and financial
pressure and built what the public wanted,
whether Cape Cod colonial or Tudor
Gothic. There were no other choices. Only
Griffin and Mahony were safely out of the
country. And this, the decade of the 1920s,
was one of the most prosperous building
periods in American history.

The demise of the Prairie School finds
parallels in the fate of each of the European design movements that existed at the
turn of the century. Yet the life of the
Prairie School had been as long or longer,
and certainly more productive, than any
of the others. The Prairie School had its
impact on Europe, Australia, and America,
directly affecting the development of what
we know as modern architecture. It has
even undergone revival, as in the Ranch
Style homes of the 1950s and 1960s. Yet
more importantly it has, largely through
Wright, left us concepts of great signifi-
cance. One is a philosophically based
system of design: organic architecture.

Another is the idea of space that is created
by defining rather than enclosing it, a
space which can vary in function accord-
ing to the needs and the activities of the
user. The implications of this have only
begun to be understood by the architectural profession, and are still not appreciated by the layman, thus leaving us with a
vast, largely untapped resource for future
generations.

The buildings of the Prairie School, in
spite of their international impact and
continuing influence, were very respectful
of their own time and place and very
much American. They were not fanciful
inventions for the sake of being different,
but rather combined the best ideas, both
from high art and the vernacular, that
American architecture had to offer. Re-
sponsive to the lessons (and romanticism)
of nature, and to the modernity of the
machine, these buildings, the many hun-
dreds of them, have more than stood the
test of time and continue their useful
service with little or no need of modifica-
tion. Nestling quietly into the landscape,
where they seem to belong, they enrich the
quality of life for all who know them, and
leave us with an abundant inheritance of
ideas and principles for the future.

Footnotes

1. Edgar Kaufmann and Ben Raeburn, eds., *Frank Lloyd Wright: Writings and Buildings* (New York: 1960), p. 65.

2. Leonard K. Eaton, *Two Chicago Architects and Their Clients: Frank Lloyd Wright and Howard Van Doren Shaw* (Cambridge, Mass.: 1969), and Eugene R. Streich, "An Original-Owner Interview Survey of Frank Lloyd Wright's Residential Architecture," in H. Allen Brooks, ed., *Writings on Wright: Selected Comment on Frank Lloyd Wright* (Cambridge, Mass.: 1981), pp. 35–45.

3. Frank Lloyd Wright, "In the Cause of Architecture," *Architectural Record*, 23 (March 1908): 158.

4. In figure 1, Silsbee's chapel, observe the concurrence of horizontals associated with the band of contiguous north-side windows. The masonry base (water table) is raised to coincide with the window sills (and because it is higher than usual it emphasizes horizontality) while the tops of the windows coincide with the eaves of the roof. Thus, the windows do not create a secondary set of horizontals or have the appearance of being punched into the wall; rather they seem to glide on upper and lower tracks. Wright applied this lesson in the M. H. Lowell project (pl. 10).

5. The house is located at 428 Forest Avenue, corner of Chicago Avenue, Oak Park, Illinois, and is now owned by the Frank Lloyd Wright Home and Studio Foundation, which sponsors tours several afternoons each week. Nearby is Unity Temple (corner of Lake Street and Kenilworth Avenue), which has occasional tours, but because architecture is always best appreciated in its intended context it is obviously preferable to participate in Sunday services. Both buildings are designated as National Historic Landmarks.

6. An analysis of Wright's process of self-education, which culminated in the building of the Winslow House, will be found in my "Frank Lloyd Wright—Toward Maturity of Style: 1887–1893," *AA Files: Annals of the Architectural Association*, 1, No. 2 (July 1982): 44–49.

7. *Architectural Record*, op. cit., p. 156.

8. Sullivan closely allied himself with the younger generation by giving talks, writing articles, and participating in certain of their activities. He spoke on 30 May 1899 at the Chicago Architectural Club on "The Principles of Architectural Design" and three days later his paper "The Modern Phase of Architecture" was read by Webster Tomlinson (see letterhead, pl. 10) at the founding convention of the Architectural League of America, an organization largely fostered by the Chicago club. The second convention was held a year later at the Auditorium Building in Chicago, where "the feature of the morning . . . was the ovation to Mr. Sullivan, who was present in the audience as a spectator and called upon to address the convention. He was evidently the master, and, as one of the later speakers (Frank Lloyd Wright) expressed it, they the disciples, and he was greeted with continued and continued applause, which only stopped as he began his extemporaneous remarks" (*American Architect and Building News*, 68 [1900]: 87). At the same convention Sullivan delivered his celebrated address "The Young Man in Architecture," which, expanded and rewritten, was published serially (1901–2) as *Kindergarten Chats* and subsequently as a book.

9. Birth and death dates are provided only for those designers whose work is actually illustrated or discussed herein.

10. See H. Allen Brooks, "Frank Lloyd Wright and the Wasmuth Drawings," *Art Bulletin*, 48 (1966): 193–202, where the drawings and their authorship is discussed and a comparison between drawings and their photographic sources is illustrated.

11. Brooks, *Writings on Wright*, op. cit., pp. 129–30.

12. A much fuller and more completely documented discussion of Wrightian space will be found in my "Wright and the Destruction of the Box," *Writings on Wright*, op. cit., pp. 175–88.

13. David A. Hanks has researched the records of the Niedecken-Walbridge Co. to establish their role vis-à-vis Wright; my analysis is indebted to his findings. See David A. Hanks, *The Decorative Designs of Frank Lloyd Wright* (New York: 1979).

Bibliographic Note

No other book covers precisely the same area as this. The closest, however, is my own *The Prairie School: Frank Lloyd Wright and His Midwest Contemporaries* (Toronto: University of Toronto Press, 1972; New York: W. W. Norton, 1976), which, though discussing the movement in depth, treats Wright's built work only in passing in order to concentrate upon his lesser-known colleagues. A companion publication is *Prairie School Architecture: Studies from 'The Western Architect,'* H. Allen Brooks, ed., (Toronto: University of Toronto Press, 1975; New York: Van Nostrand Reinhold, 1983), which includes fifteen well-illustrated articles by or about the Prairie School architects, that appeared during the years after 1911, plus brief biographies and an introduction. Except for Wright, only Griffin has been the subject of a full-length monograph: Donald Leslie Johnson, *The Architecture of Walter Burley Griffin* (Melbourne: Macmillan, 1977). His architecture, depicted in Marion Mahony Griffin's superb drawings, is beautifully reproduced in David T. Van Zanten, ed., *Walter Burley Griffin: Selected Drawings* (Palos Park, Illinois: Prairie School Press, 1970). For the others, only shorter essays are available: *Barry Byrne and John Lloyd Wright: Architecture and Design* by Sally Kitt Chappell and Ann Van Zanten (Chicago: Chicago Historical Society, 1982) and *The Domestic Scene (1897–1927): George M. Niedecken, Interior Architect* by Cheryl Robertson et al. (Milwaukee: Milwaukee Art Museum, 1981). The *Prairie School*

Review, a quarterly founded in 1964 but now defunct, published numerous articles on this subject.

Frank Lloyd Wright was long neglected by his countrymen. Not until 1942, when he had reached the age of seventy-five, did the first book about him in English appear (books in German, Dutch, and French had been published since 1910). Ten years before, he had written *An Autobiography* (1932, 1943, and 1976 editions), which is basic reading though not yet available in paperback. More accessible is his *The Future of Architecture* (various editions beginning in 1953), an inexpensive anthology that provides excellent insights into the man and his work, as does *The Natural House* (New York: Horizon, 1954). *A Testament* (New York: Horizon, 1957) is the autobiography he published at the age of ninety.

Biographies and architectural histories concerning Wright are no longer in short supply, a selection of six being alphabetically listed here. H. Allen Brooks, ed., *Writings on Wright: Selected Comment on Frank Lloyd Wright* (Cambridge, Mass.: M.I.T. Press, 1981) is my attempt to achieve, through the extensive use of other people's words, a deeper, more sympathetic insight into Wright's personality and process of design as well as to learn, from the homeowners themselves, precisely what is unique about living in a Wright-designed house. Henry-Russell Hitchcock, *In the Nature of Materials* (New York: Duell, Sloan and Pearce, 1942), is the first and still essential work on Wright, being particularly useful as a reference source for illustrations and plans. Grant C. Manson, *Frank Lloyd Wright to 1910* (New York: Reinhold, 1958), is an excellent in-depth study of his early prairie years, but unfortunately it terminates before they were over. The other three books are all entitled *Frank Lloyd Wright*. That by Vincent Scully, Jr. (New York: George Braziller, 1960) is short and stimulating; that by Norris Kelly Smith (Englewood Cliffs, N.J.: Prentice-Hall, 1966) is a thoughtful and provocative account that ends in the 1930s; Robert C. Twombly's (New York: John Wiley, 1979) is the most complete and authoritative concerning biographical data, yet it is relatively less involved with architecture. For Wright's ornamental work and house furnishings the most definitive study is David A. Hanks, *The Decorative Designs of Frank Lloyd Wright* (New York: E. P. Dutton, 1979). All except Twombly are now in paperback. Anyone seeking a more extensive list is referred to Robert L. Sweeney, *Frank Lloyd Wright: An Annotated Bibliography* (Los Angeles: Hennessey, 1978), with its over two thousand entries.

Guides

There is no guide book specifically for the Prairie School. Wright's total built work is listed in William Allin Storrer, *The Architecture of Frank Lloyd Wright: A Complete Catalogue* (Cambridge, Mass.: M.I.T. Press, 1974). For other architects see my own volume, *The Prairie School* (Toronto: University of Toronto Press, 1972), wherein I indexed each illustrated building by town or city and included the street address with the caption. Area guides are more detailed but also more limiting because they eliminate all buildings outside their rigid geographic boundary. For Oak Park (but excluding contiguous River Forest) see Paul E. Sprague, *Guide to Frank Lloyd Wright and Prairie School Architecture in Oak Park* (Oak Park, Ill.: 1976). State guides vary in usefulness, the most exemplary being David Gebhard and Tom Martinson, *A Guide to the Architecture of Minnesota* (Minneapolis: University of Minnesota Press, 1978). Yet it is always rewarding and fun to visit specialized bookshops such as that at the Art Institute of Chicago, or the Prairie Avenue Bookstore on South Dearborn Street in Chicago, or the little shop at the Frank Lloyd Wright Home and Studio Foundation in Oak Park, Illinois.

Plates

1. **Frank Lloyd Wright**

Frank Thomas House, Oak Park,
    Illinois, 1901

Perspective

Pen and ink, watercolor on paper
    20.3 × 54.4 cm. (sight)

Pacific Northwest Collection, Univer-
    sity of Washington Libraries, Seattle

2. Frank Lloyd Wright

Susan Lawrence Dana House,
   Springfield, Illinois, 1903

Dining room

Pencil, pastels, and washes on brown
   paper; 63.5 × 51.6 cm.

Avery Library, Columbia University,
   New York

Much of the decoration in the Dana
House was based upon stylized natural forms: the prairie sumac for the art
glass windows and an abstracted but-
terfly motif in the hanging lamps. The
dining room mural, slightly modified
in execution, was painted by George
M. Niedecken. This was the first of
Wright's many collaborations with the
Milwaukee-based interior designer.

3. **Frank Lloyd Wright**

Unity Temple, Oak Park, Illinois,
   1906

Photograph: H. A. Brooks

4. **Edgewood Place, River Forest, Illinois**

Photograph: H. A. Brooks

A typical suburban house setting in the American Midwest with towering elm trees along the street, the houses set well back in the flat lot, and without restrictive hedges, plantings, or fences to form a barrier against neighbors and pedestrians. On the right is William Drummond's own house of 1910; to the left, Frank Lloyd Wright's Isabel Roberts House of 1908 (brick resurfacing later).

5. **Frank Lloyd Wright**

Taliesin, Spring Green, Wisconsin, begun 1911; rebuilt 1914 and 1925

Photograph: H. A. Brooks

MR. FRANK LLOYD WRIGHT'S GIFT TO THE DEPARTMENT

6. **Frank Lloyd Wright**

Project: Sherman M. Booth House,
Glencoe, Illinois, ca. 1911–13

Perspective

Pencil and colored pencils on Japanese
paper; 35.2 × 79.6 cm.

Chicago Architecture Foundation

Wright took advantage of this site on
the edge of a steep ravine to create one
of his most dramatic designs. The plan
is shaped like a pinwheel, its wings
fanning out in different directions
from the central block, which contains
a two-story living room. The house
was built in 1915 to a modified design.

7. **Frank Lloyd Wright**

Henry J. Allen House, Wichita, Kansas, 1917

Dining room light standard

Pencil and colored pencils on tracing paper; 37.3 × 19.2 cm.

Cooper-Hewitt Museum: Smithsonian Regents' Acquisitions Fund and Friends of Drawings and Prints

8. **Frank Lloyd Wright**

"January" cover design for *Liberty*
   magazine, 1926–27

Pencil and colored pencils on paper;
   36 × 61.4 cm.

Private Collection

1. **Frank Lloyd Wright**

Frank Lloyd Wright House,
    Oak Park, Illinois, 1889

Photograph courtesy The Frank
    Lloyd Wright Home and Studio
    Foundation, Oak Park, Illinois

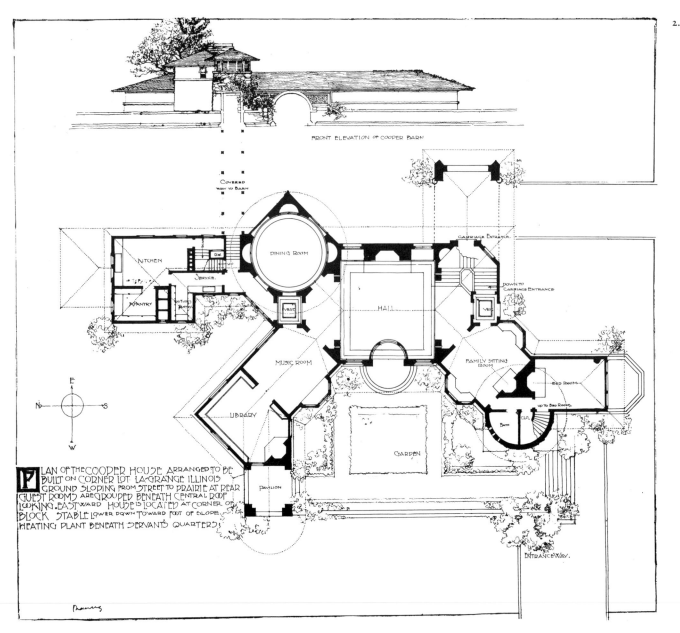

FRONT ELEVATION OF COOPER BARN

2. **Frank Lloyd Wright**

Project: Cooper House, La Grange, Illinois, ca. 1887

Plan, and elevation of stables

Pen and ink on tracing paper; 121.9 × 121.9 cm.

The Frank Lloyd Wright Memorial Foundation

PLAN OF THE COOPER HOUSE ARRANGED TO BE BUILT ON CORNER LOT LA·GRANGE ILLINOIS GROUND SLOPING FROM STREET TO PRAIRIE AT REAR GUEST ROOMS ARE GROUPED BENEATH CENTRAL ROOF LOOKING EASTWARD HOUSE IS LOCATED AT CORNER OF BLOCK STABLE LOWER DOWN TOWARD FOOT OF SLOPE HEATING PLANT BENEATH SERVANTS QUARTERS

4. Louis H. Sullivan; tracing by Frank Lloyd Wright

Wainwright Tomb, St. Louis, Missouri, 1892

Ornamental gate

Pen and ink on linen; 70 × 60.2 cm.

Avery Library, Columbia University, New York

The six years, 1887 to 1893, that Wright spent in the office of Adler and Sullivan were instrumental in shaping the direction of his early career. Hired at first to prepare working drawings from Sullivan's ornament sketches, Wright soon became the firm's chief draftsman and later assumed responsibility for the design of its residential work.

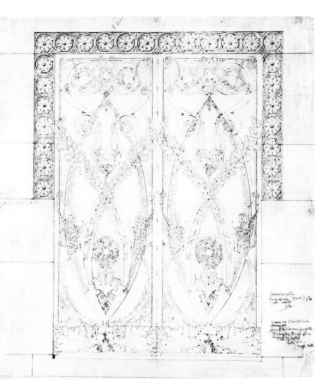

3. Louis H. Sullivan

Wainwright Tomb, St. Louis, Missouri, ca. 1892

Drawing for a limestone frieze

Pencil on paper; 39.8 × 63 cm. (sight)

The University of Michigan Museum of Art, transfer from The College of Architecture and Design

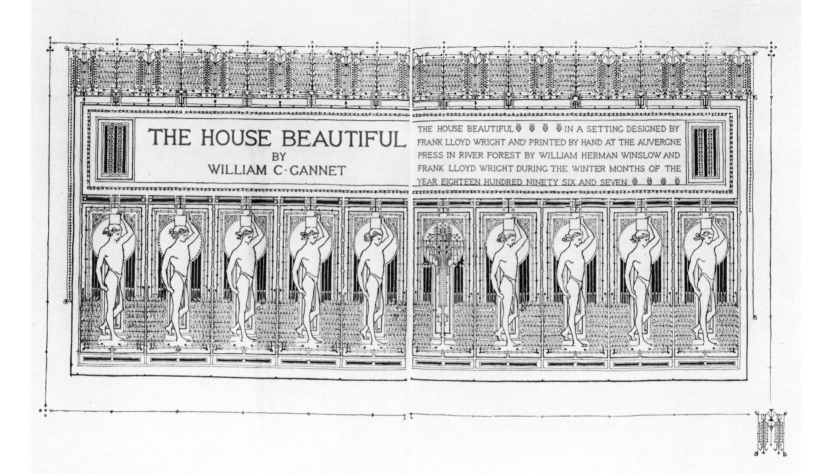

5. Frank Lloyd Wright

The House Beautiful, by William C.
   Gannet, 1897

Title page

Pen and black and red ink on paper;
   35 × 59 cm.

Chicago Historical Society

6. **Frank Lloyd Wright**

William H. Winslow House,
    River Forest, Illinois, 1894

Photograph courtesy The Museum of
    Modern Art, New York

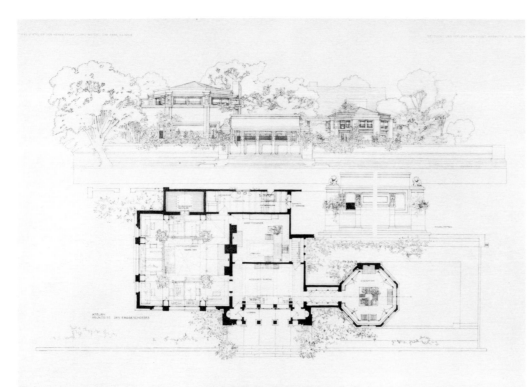

7. Frank Lloyd Wright Studio

Library (from the *Chicago Architecture Club Annual* of 1902)

Kelmscott Gallery, Chicago, Illinois

8. Frank Lloyd Wright

Frank Lloyd Wright Studio, Oak Park, Illinois, 1898

Plan and elevation

Pl. VI, *Ausgeführte Bauten und Entwürfe von Frank Lloyd Wright.* Berlin: Ernst Wasmuth, 1910

Lithograph in brown ink; 39.8 × 64.3 cm.

Avery Library, Columbia University, New York

Wright made a number of significant additions to his own house, including a wing to the east, containing on its second floor a tall, barrel-vaulted playroom for his children. The fireplace mural, illustrating a tale from the *Arabian Nights*, was executed by Orlando Giannini, an artist who also manufactured art glass for Wright and other Prairie School architects.

The last major addition was the architect's own studio, housing an office, drafting room, and library. This, which he called "an early study in articulation," reflected not only the considerable size to which Wright's practice had by then expanded, but also his belief in the integration of home and workplace.

9. Frank Lloyd Wright

Frank Lloyd Wright House, Oak Park, Illinois, 1889

Playroom addition of 1895

Avery Library, Columbia University, New York

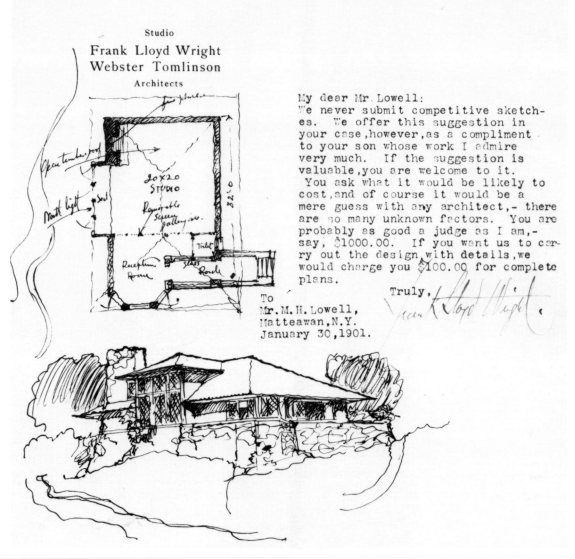

Studio

Frank Lloyd Wright
Webster Tomlinson
Architects

20×20
STUDIO

My dear Mr. Lowell:
We never submit competitive sketches. We offer this suggestion in
your case, however, as a compliment
to your son whose work I admire
very much. If the suggestion is
valuable, you are welcome to it.
You ask what it would be likely to
cost, and of course it would be a
mere guess with any architect,- there
are so many unknown factors. You are
probably as good a judge as I am,-
say, $1000.00. If you want us to car-
ry out the design with details, we
would charge you $100.00 for complete
plans.

Truly,

To
Mr. M. H. Lowell,
Matteawan, N.Y.
January 30, 1901.

10. **Frank Lloyd Wright**

Letter to Mr. M. H. Lowell,
Matteawan, New York, 1901

Pen and black ink on paper;
22.3 × 22.3 cm.

Avery Library, Columbia University,
New York

11. Frank Lloyd Wright

Project: "A Home in a Prairie Town," 1900

Perspective

Pl. XIII, *Ausgeführte Bauten und Entwürfe von Frank Lloyd Wright.* Berlin: Ernst Wasmuth, 1910

Lithograph in gray ink; 39.8 × 64.3 cm.

Avery Library, Columbia University, New York

Wright's prairie houses, the first of which date from 1900–1901, demonstrate his concern that a building should respond to its setting—in this case the broad plains of the American Midwest. These designs are characterized by long, unbroken wall surfaces, continuous bands of leaded casement windows, and low, spreading roofs which, Wright explained, would provide protection from extremes of weather and "give a sense of shelter in the look of a building."

He extended the lines of the house into the landscape itself with terraces, pergolas, and covered porches, so that it "began to associate with the ground and became natural to its prairie site."

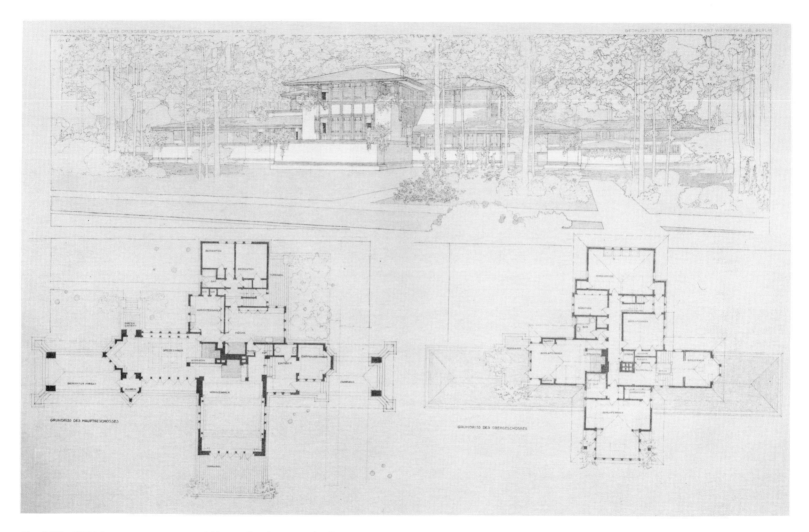

12. **Frank Lloyd Wright**

Ward W. Willits House, Highland
Park, Illinois, 1902

Ground plan and perspective

Pl. XXV, *Ausgeführte Bauten und
Entwürfe von Frank Lloyd Wright.*
Berlin: Ernst Wasmuth, 1910

Lithograph in brown and yellow ink;
39.8 × 64.3 cm.

Avery Library, Columbia University,
New York

13. **Walter Burley Griffin**

William H. Emery House, Elmhurst, Illinois, 1901–2

Photograph: H. A. Brooks

Shortly after graduating in architecture from the University of Illinois, Walter Burley Griffin joined the Oak Park Studio in 1901. He remained there until 1905, when he left to establish his own practice. Griffin's early works reflect his taste for closed, somewhat sculptural form—apparent in the heavy, gabled roofs and thick corner piers of the Emery House. In contrast to Wright's preference for horizontal extension, Griffin tended to develop his designs vertically, creating compact, yet spatially unified interiors by interleafing the rooms one into the next at split levels.

14. Frank Lloyd Wright

Susan Lawrence Dana House,
  Springfield, Illinois, 1903

Perspective

Pl. XXXIa, *Ausgeführte Bauten und
  Entwürfe von Frank Lloyd Wright.*
  Berlin: Ernst Wasmuth, 1910

Lithograph in brown ink; 39.8 × 64.3
  cm.

Avery Library, Columbia University,
  New York

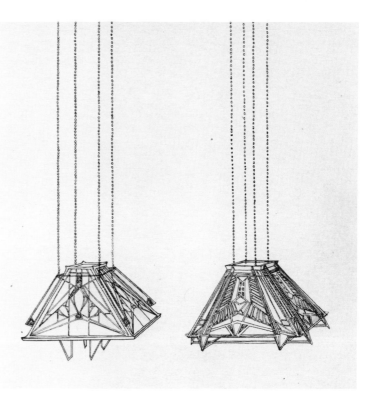

15. **Susan Lawrence Dana House**

Dining room window

Leaded glass, wood frame;
117.5 × 80 cm.

Greenville College, The Richard W.
Bock Sculpture Collection, Greenville, Illinois

16. **George M. Niedecken**

Lawrence Demmer House,
Milwaukee, Wisconsin

Hanging lamps, 1907–16

Pen and ink, watercolor on paper;
25 × 28 cm.

Private Collection

17. Frank Lloyd Wright

Darwin D. Martin House, Buffalo, New York, 1904–5

Buffalo and Erie County Historical Society

Between 1903 and 1905, Wright designed a complex of six buildings for the Martin family. The largest, the Martin House itself, faced the Jewett Parkway front of their Buffalo property. To the rear, Wright placed the Barton House, for Martin's sister and brother-in-law, as well as a gardener's cottage, garage, greenhouse, and conservatory, connected to the main house by a pergola.

In his own house, Martin granted Wright complete control over the design, interior and exterior. Its plan is an amplified version of the architect's published project of 1900, "A Home in a Prairie Town." The major living spaces, now somewhat vandalized, contained a full complement of his furniture, lighting fixtures, and art glass.

18. Darwin D. Martin House

Reception room

Collection Centre Canadien d'Architecture/Canadian Centre for Architecture, Montreal

19. Darwin D. Martin House

Plan

Architectural Record, 63 (1928)

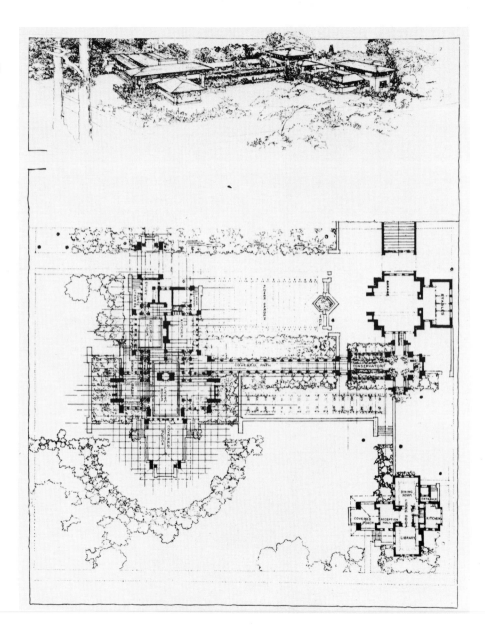

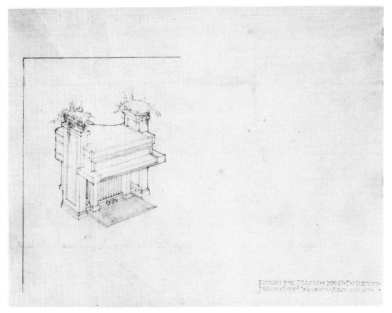

20. Darwin D. Martin House

Piano, ca. 1905

Pencil on paper
26 × 27 cm.

Kelmscott Gallery, Chicago, Illinois

21. Darwin D. Martin House

Table lamp

Brass, leaded glass;
43.8 × 24.8 × 31.8 cm.

Darwin D. Martin House, School of
Architecture and Environmental
Design, State University of New
York at Buffalo

22. Darwin D. Martin House

Wall sconce, 1905

Pencil on paper
55.2 × 83.9 cm.

Kelmscott Gallery, Chicago, Illinois

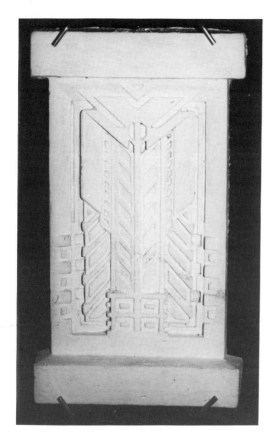

23. Richard W. Bock for Frank Lloyd Wright

Larkin Company Administration Building

Pier relief model

Plaster; 56.5 × 40.7 × 6.4 cm.

Greenville College, The Richard W. Bock Sculpture Collection, Greenville, Illinois

24. Frank Lloyd Wright

Larkin Company Administration
Building, Buffalo, New York, 1904

Buffalo and Erie County Historical
Society

The commission for the Larkin
Building, Wright's first important
commercial design, came through the
recommendation of Darwin D. Martin, an executive of the manufactur-
ing and mail order company. In
comparison to most contemporary
work, the planning of the interior
was remarkably open, with the office
spaces arranged in tiers around a
central court. The building featured a
number of innovations, among them
a system of air filtration and steel
furniture designed by the architect.
Services such as piping, ventilation,
and the stairwells were clustered at
the corners, in the massive brick
shafts that gave the building its stark
and monumental appearance.

**25. Larkin Company Administration
Building**

Interior court

Kelmscott Gallery, Chicago, Illinois

**26. Larkin Company Administration
    Building**

Cafeteria

Harry H. Larkin, Jr.

27. Frank Lloyd Wright

Side chair, ca. 1904

Oak, upholstered seat;
103 × 38 × 47.7 cm.

Sydney and Frances Lewis
Foundation

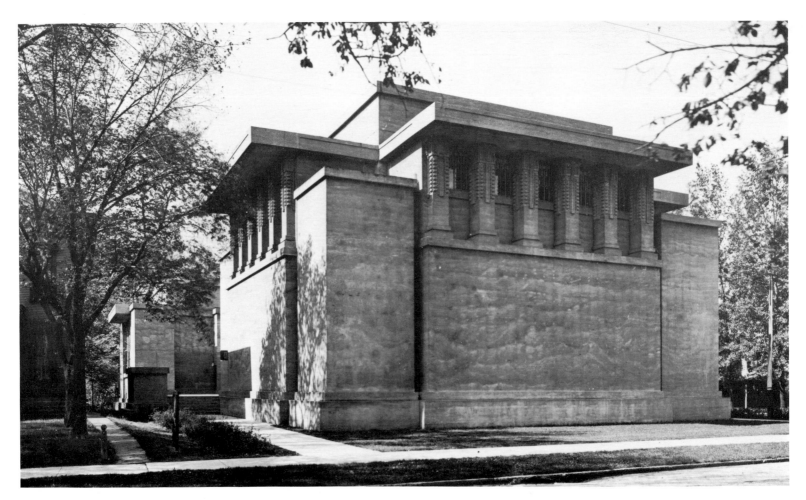

28. Frank Lloyd Wright

Unity Temple, Oak Park, Illinois,
 1906–8

Photograph courtesy The Museum of
 Modern Art, New York

At Unity Temple, the disposition of
interior spaces, the "sense of the
room," as Wright called it, is clearly
evident on the exterior, which steps
down from the tall, top-lit volume of
the auditorium, to the short, bal-
conied crossarms, and finally to the
piers containing the stairwells at each
corner. The same theme was repeated
on a smaller scale in the adjacent
parish house. This design was executed in poured concrete, Wright's
first extensive use of this material.

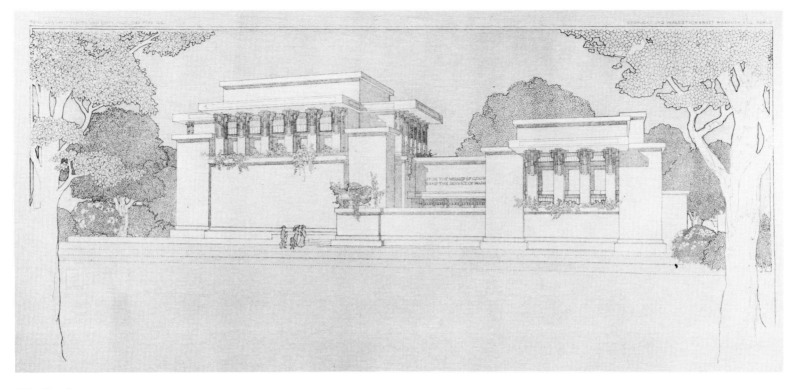

29. Unity Temple

Perspective

Pl. LXIII, *Ausgeführte Bauten und Entwürfe von Frank Lloyd Wright.* Berlin: Ernst Wasmuth, 1910

Lithograph in brown ink; 39.8 × 64.3 cm.

Avery Library, Columbia University, New York

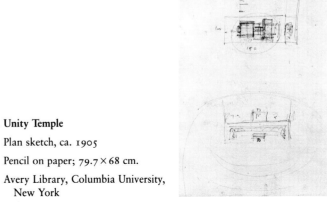

30. Unity Temple

Plan sketch, ca. 1905

Pencil on paper; 79.7 × 68 cm.

Avery Library, Columbia University, New York

32. Frank Lloyd Wright

Project: Summer Cottage for Darwin
    D. Martin, ca. 1908

Perspective

Pen and brown ink on paper;
    25.4 × 68.6 cm.

Kelmscott Gallery, Chicago, Illinois

**31. Robert C. Spencer and
    Horace S. Powers**

Edward W. McCready House,
    Oak Park, Illinois, 1907

Photograph courtesy Historic
    American Buildings Survey

33. Frank Lloyd Wright

Avery Coonley House, Riverside,
Illinois, 1908–9

Living room

Collection Centre Canadien d'Archi-
tecture/Canadian Centre for Architecture, Montreal

The Coonley living room is a magnif-
icent realization of the principles
Wright sought to express in the
design of his prairie houses. The
stained oak strips on the ceiling
articulate the wood frame of the
structure and echo the sloping planes
of the hipped roof above, giving
dramatic shape to the space as well
as a feeling of shelter. On three sides
of the room, bands of casement
windows provide views of the
garden, while on the fourth, this
sense of openness is extended in
pictorial terms by the birch tree
mural. This was painted by George
M. Niedecken, whose firm was retained by Wright to supervise the
manufacture and installation of the
furnishings.

**34. George M. Niedecken for Frank
Lloyd Wright**

Avery Coonley House

Desk for rear guest room, ca. 1908

Pen and brown ink, watercolors on
tracing paper; 27.7 × 39.4 cm.

Art Institute of Chicago

35. Louis H. Sullivan

Henry Babson House, Riverside, Illinois, 1906–8

Brickbuilder, 19 (1910)

One of Sullivan's few residential designs, executed in collaboration with his associate George Elmslie, the Babson House possesses a number of features which also characterize the work of his younger contemporaries: low, horizontally disposed massing, accentuated by gently pitched roofs with broad eaves and long, covered porches. Babson later employed several Prairie School artists and architects—Purcell and Elmslie, George Niedecken, and Alfonso Iannelli—to redecorate the house or design other buildings on his property.

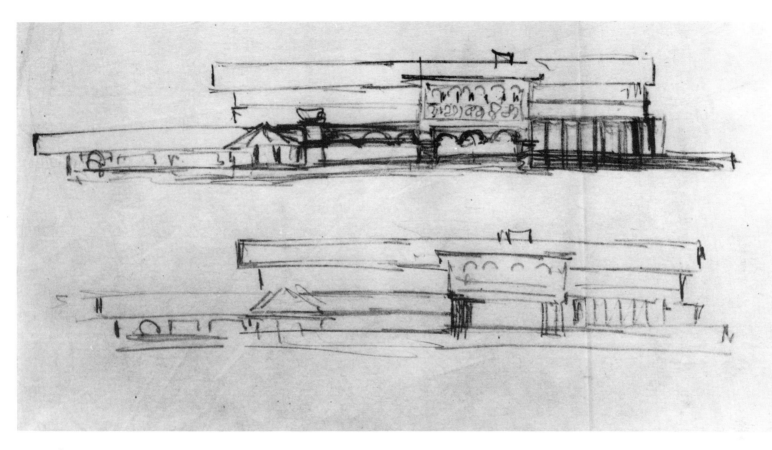

36. **Henry Babson House**

Elevation sketches, ca. 1906

Pencil on paper; 11.5 × 21.5 cm.

Private Collection

37. Frank Lloyd Wright

Frederick C. Robie House, Chicago,
  Illinois, 1908–9

Collection Centre Canadien d'Archi-
  tecture/Canadian Centre for Architecture, Montreal

38. Frederick C. Robie House

Ground- and first-floor plans

Ausgeführte Bauten von Frank Lloyd Wright. Berlin: Ernst Wasmuth, 1911

Like many of his designs for narrow suburban lots, the plan of the Robie House unfolds along a single axis, stepping downward and outward from the massive central core of the chimney in a complex series of over-lapping horizontal planes. Here wall surfaces have been reduced to a minimum (now merely short spurs at the corners carrying the steel beams which run the length of the house), replaced by the more functionally articulate forms of Wright's new architectural vocabulary: broad, sheltering roofs; low balconies; and tall casements—which together provide both privacy and a sense of openness for the long, narrow living spaces within.

The interior of the Robie House is a particularly noteworthy example of Wright's insistence that the forms, materials, and patterns of furniture and decoration be determined by their architectural setting.

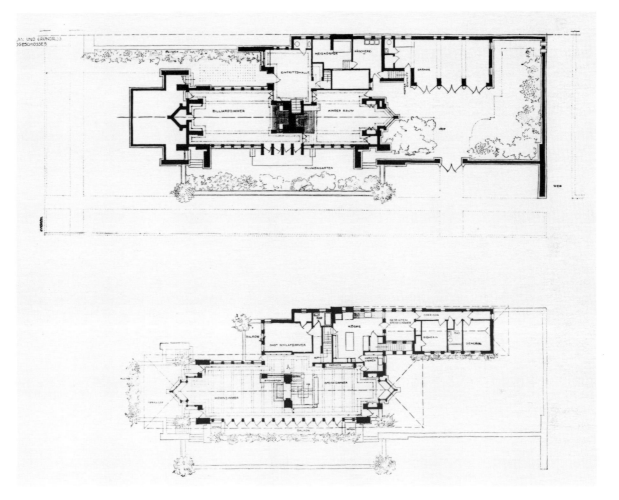

40. George M. Niedecken for Frank Lloyd Wright

Frederick C. Robie House

Design for living room decorations, 1909–10

Pencil and watercolors on buff paper; 26.1 × 79.4 cm.

Prairie Archives Collection, Milwaukee Art Museum, Gift of Mr. and Mrs. Robert L. Jacobson

39. Frederick C. Robie House

Dining room

Collection Centre Canadien d'Architecture/Canadian Centre for Architecture, Montreal

41. George M. Niedecken for Frank Lloyd Wright

Frederick C. Robie House

Living room lamp, ca. 1910

Pencil on paper; 29.9 × 23 cm.

Prairie Archives Collection, Milwaukee Art Museum, Gift of Mr. and Mrs. Robert L. Jacobson

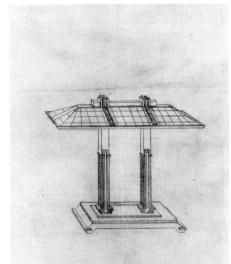

42. Frederick C. Robie House

Window

Leaded glass, wood frame;
124.5 × 76.8 cm.

The David and Alfred Smart Gallery,
the University of Chicago

43. Frank Lloyd Wright

P. A. Beachy House, Oak Park, Illinois, 1906

Dining room chair

Oak, upholstered seat;
116.8 × 35.6 × 45.8 cm.

Sydney and Frances Lewis Collection

44. Andrew Willatzen and Francis Barry Byrne

Perspective

C. H. Clarke House, The Highlands,
near Seattle, Washington, 1909

Pen and black ink, watercolors, pencil on paper; 29.2 × 79.5 cm.

Pacific Northwest Collection, University of Washington Libraries,
Seattle

45. Walter Burley Griffin

F. B. Carter House, Evanston,
Illinois, 1910

Photograph: H. A. Brooks

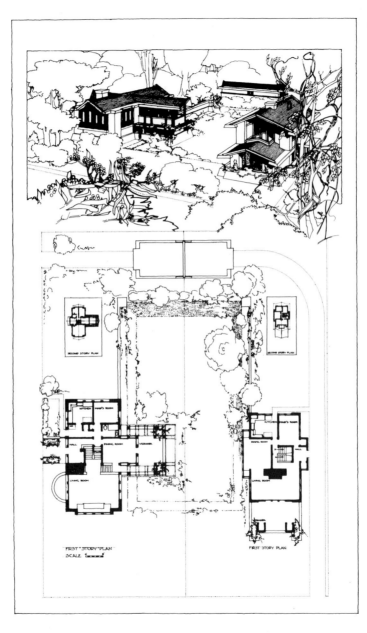

46. Walter Burley Griffin; rendering by Marion Mahony Griffin

Hurd Comstock Houses, Evanston, Illinois, 1912

Perspective and plans

Pen and black ink on linen; 97.8 × 55.9 cm.

Mary and Leigh Block Gallery, Northwestern University, Gift of Marion Mahony Griffin

47. Frank Lloyd Wright

Taliesin, Spring Green, Wisconsin, begun 1911; rebuilt 1914 and 1925

Photograph: H. A. Brooks

Taliesin, Wright's principal residence after 1911, combined several functions: home, architectural studio, and working farm. The Welsh name he gave to it, which translated means "Shining Brow," symbolized for him one important aspect of the design. The house does not dominate its setting, but rather seems to grow naturally from it. "For me," he wrote in *An Autobiography*, "its elevation is the modeling of the hills, the weaving and the fabric that clings to them."

48. Taliesin, Spring Green, Wisconsin

Living room, 1925

Photograph: Hedrich-Blessing Ltd.

49. Purcell, Feick and Elmslie

Edward W. Decker House,
Holdridge, Lake Minnetonka,
Minnesota, 1912–13

Northwest Architectural Archives,
University of Minnesota Libraries,
Minneapolis

50. Edward W. Decker House

Plan

Architectural Record, 30 (1915)

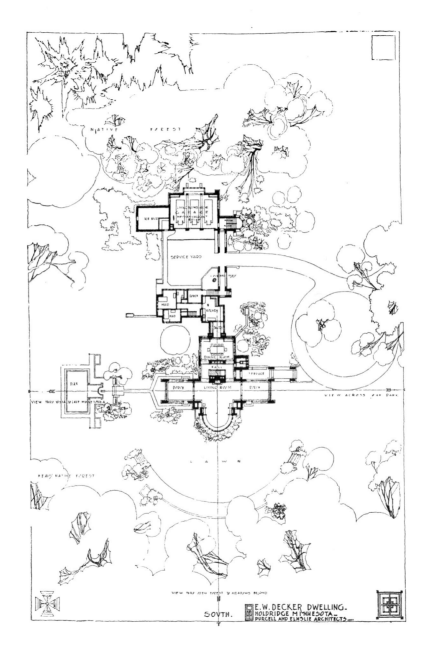

51. **Frank Lloyd Wright**

Mrs. Thomas H. Gale House,
Oak Park, Illinois, 1909

Perspective

Detail, Pl. XLV, *Ausgeführte Bauten
und Entwürfe von Frank Lloyd
Wright*. Berlin: Ernst Wasmuth,
1910

Lithograph in brown ink; 64.3 × 39.8
cm.

Avery Library, Columbia University,
New York

52. **William E. Drummond**

First project: Dexter M. Ferry, Jr.,
   House, Grosse Point, Michigan,
   1910

Front elevation

Pen and ink on paper; 50.2 × 85.1
   cm.

Chicago Architecture Foundation

53. Frank Lloyd Wright

Avery Coonley Playhouse, Riverside, Illinois, 1912

Collection Centre Canadien d'Architecture/Canadian Centre for Architecture, Montreal

54. Purcell, Feick and Elmslie

Edna S. Purcell House, Minneapolis, Minnesota, 1913

Front elevation

Pencil and colored pencils on paper; 24.2 × 22.3 cm.

Dr. David Gebhard

While it is true that Wright and Sullivan provided both a formal and theoretical model for their younger contemporaries, the most significant contributions to the movement after 1910 were made by others—Griffin, Byrne, Drummond, and especially Purcell and Elmslie. Purcell's own house is one of the finest of this firm's residential works, and reflects in its plan, materials, and decorative detailing many of the characteristic features of Prairie School design.

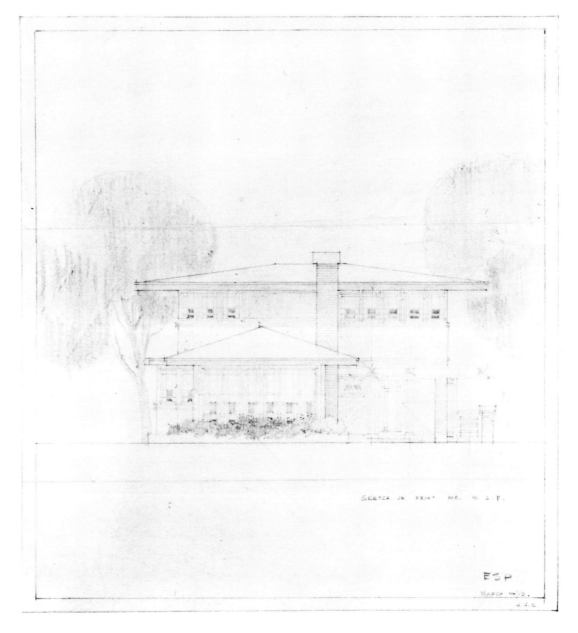

55. Edna S. Purcell House

Living room fireplace wall

Pencil and washes on canvas;
16.6 × 26.6 cm.

Dr. David Gebhard

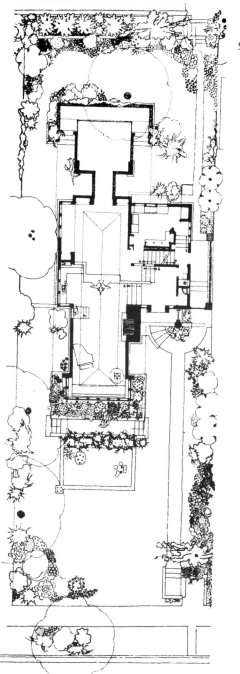

56. Edna S. Purcell House

Plan

Northwest Architectural Archives,
   University of Minnesota Libraries,
   Minneapolis

58. George G. Elmslie

Design for chancel railing, n.d.

Pen and black ink, red and blue
  pastel on paper; 17.8 × 25.5 cm.

Mr. and Mrs. Roger G. Kennedy

57. **Edna S. Purcell House**

Writing nook

Private Collection

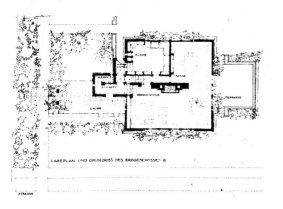

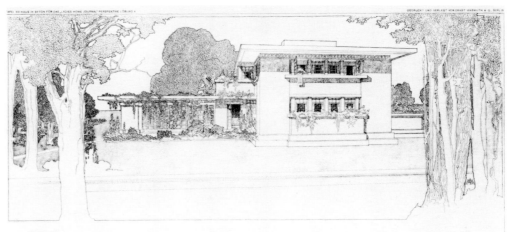

59. Frank Lloyd Wright

Project: "A Fireproof House for $5,000," 1906

Perspective and plan

Pl. XIV, *Ausgeführte Bauten und Entwürfe von Frank Lloyd Wright.* Berlin: Ernst Wasmuth, 1910

Lithograph in brown ink; 39.8 × 64.3 cm.

Avery Library, Columbia University, New York

This small foursquare design for a single-family home is illustrative of Wright's recurrent interest in providing an artistic solution to the problem of economical housing. It was to be built of concrete; hence its shapes—most notably the broad corner piers and the slab roof—were to some extent determined by what Wright felt were the characteristic properties of the material. The project was remarkably influential: Many Prairie School architects—Drummond, Bentley, Griffin, and even Wright's own son John—used it as a model for some of their early work.

60. **William E. Drummond**

William E. Drummond House,
     River Forest, Illinois, 1910

Photograph: H. A. Brooks

61. **William E. Drummond House**

Living room

Western Architect (1915)

62. Percy Dwight Bentley

Edward C. Bartl House, La Crosse,
Wisconsin, 1910

Photograph: H. A. Brooks

63. Walter Burley Griffin; rendering by Marion Mahony Griffin

J. G. Melson House, Mason City, Iowa, 1912

Perspective and plans

Pen and black ink on linen; 94 × 55 cm.

Mary and Leigh Block Gallery, Northwestern University, Gift of Marion Mahony Griffin

64. William E. Drummond

Gordon C. Abbott House, Hinsdale, Illinois, 1911–12

Perspective

Pen and brown ink, pencil, gouache on buff paper; 12.1 × 19.9 cm.

Chicago Architecture Foundation

65. John Lloyd Wright

Mrs. M. J. Wood House, Escondido, California, 1912

Perspective

Watercolors and pencil on paper; 26.5 × 52.2 cm.

Chicago Historical Society

66. Francis Barry Byrne

Hugh Gilmore House, Mason City,
Iowa, 1915

Perspective

Pen and black ink, pencil on linen;
85.3 × 45.4 cm.

Chicago Historical Society

FRANCIS BARRY BYRNE
ARCHITECT

67. **Francis Barry Byrne**

Dr. J. F. Clarke House, Fairfield,
Iowa, 1915

Private Collection

68. **Dr. J. F. Clarke House**

Elevations

Pen and black ink, yellow ink, pencil
on linen; 106 × 60.4 cm.

Chicago Historical Society

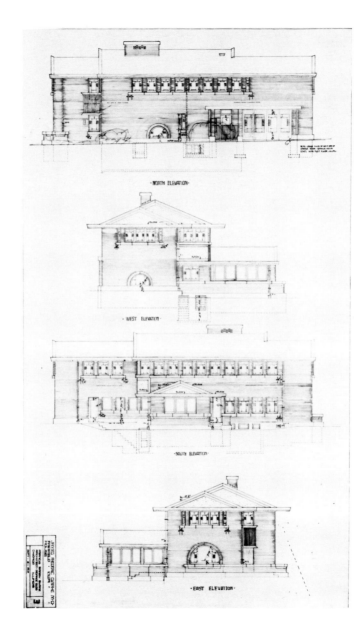

69. **Louis H. Sullivan**

National Farmers' Bank, Owatonna,
    Minnesota, 1906–8

Photograph courtesy the Richard
    Nickel Committee

70. **National Farmers' Bank, Owatonna,
    Minnesota**

Banking hall (lower portions re-
    modeled)

Photograph courtesy the Richard
    Nickel Committee

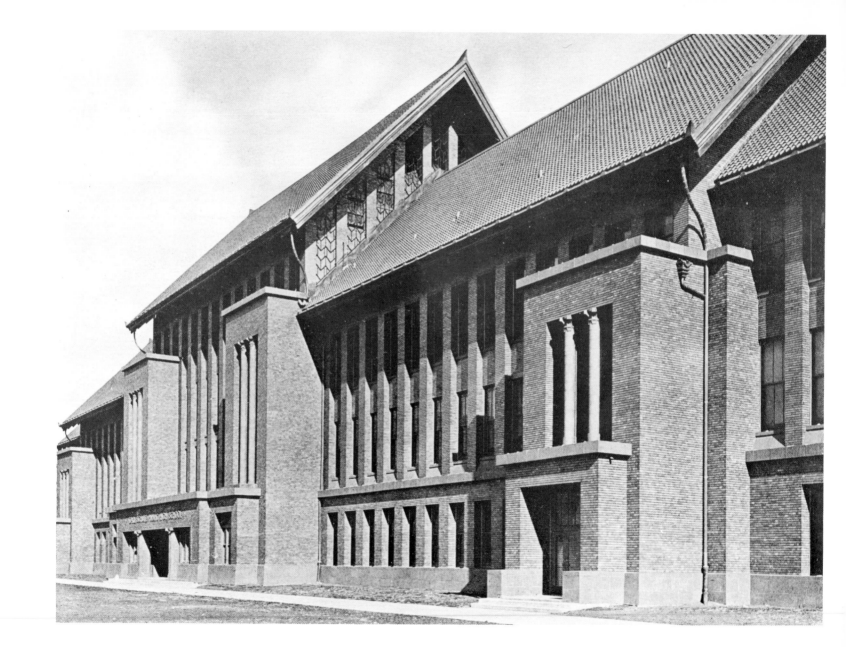

71. Dwight H. Perkins

Carl Schurz Public High School,
   Chicago, Illinois, 1908

Brickbuilder, 20 (1911)

72. Purcell, Feick and Elmslie

Merchants' Bank, Winona, Minnesota, 1911–12

Northwest Architectural Archives,
   University of Minnesota Libraries,
   Minneapolis

73. **Louis H. Sullivan**

Merchants' National Bank, Grinnell,
Iowa, 1914

Photograph courtesy the Richard
Nickel Committee

The banks, schools, and other public
buildings of the Prairie School reflect
the roots of the movement in the
progressive tradition of functionally
expressive design initiated by the
commercial architecture of the Chicago School, of which Louis Sullivan
was perhaps the most significant
figure.

74. **Merchants' National Bank, Grinnell,
Iowa**

Banking hall

Photograph: Chicago Architectural
Photographing Company

75. **Purcell and Elmslie (for William L. Steele)**

Woodbury County Courthouse, Sioux City, Iowa, 1915–17

Northwest Architectural Archives, University of Minnesota Libraries, Minneapolis

76. **Frank Lloyd Wright**

Midway Gardens, Chicago, Illinois, 1914

Exterior of Winter Garden

Wendingen, VII (1925)

77. Midway Gardens

Outdoor terraces

Wendingen, VII (1925)

Wright's design for Midway Gardens combined many elements found in his previous works, but it differed from them in its scale and complexity, as well as in the abstraction of its ornament. The repeating geometric patterns of the concrete blocks, the open rectangular frames of the towers, and even the cubic forms of the figures sculpted by Richard Bock and Alfonso Iannelli were indelibly stamped with the characteristic forms of their architectural setting.

78. Alfonso Iannelli for Frank Lloyd Wright

Midway Gardens, Chicago, Illinois

Design for "Sprite" sculpture

Pen and ink on paper; 33 × 20 cm. (sight)

Private Collection

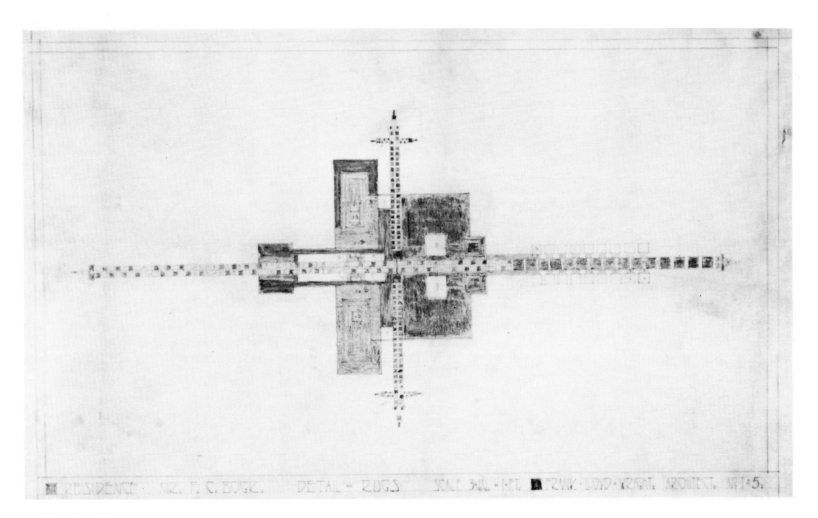

79. Frank Lloyd Wright

F. C. Bogk House, Milwaukee,
  Wisconsin, 1916

Rug detail

Pencil and colored pencils on tracing
  paper; 55.9 × 88.9 cm.

Collection Centre Canadien d'Archi-
  tecture/Canadian Centre for Architecture, Montreal

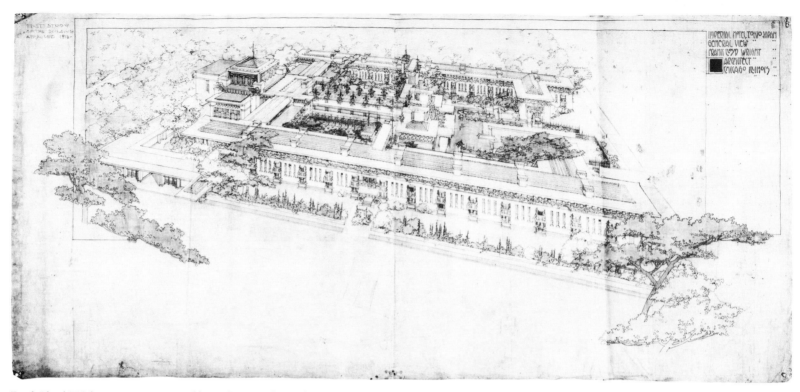

80. Frank Lloyd Wright

Imperial Hotel, Tokyo, Japan,
   1917–22

Aerial perspective

Pen and black ink, pencil, colored
   pencils on tracing cloth;
   85.2 × 189.3 cm.

The Frank Lloyd Wright Memorial
   Foundation

Unlike Midway Gardens, which was built with amazing speed, the design and construction of the Imperial Hotel occupied Wright for more than eight years. In his own account of the building, the architect laid special emphasis on the formidable technical problems he faced here and the solutions he devised to surmount them. Because the site was swampy, the foundations had to be engineered in such a way as to resist settling. The building also had to be flexible enough to withstand the shock of earthquake. Wright utilized his favorite structural device, the cantilever, isolating the load on narrow footings which floated on a bed of closely spaced concrete pins. He also "jointed" the building at intervals of sixty feet. The extraordinary amount of attention Wright devoted to these matters was justified shortly after the Imperial Hotel was completed, when it sustained almost no damage during the great earthquake of 1923.

81. Frank Lloyd Wright

Project: United States Embassy Building, Tokyo, Japan, 1914

Perspective and ground plan

Heliotype; 95 × 88 cm.

The Library of Congress, Washington, D.C.

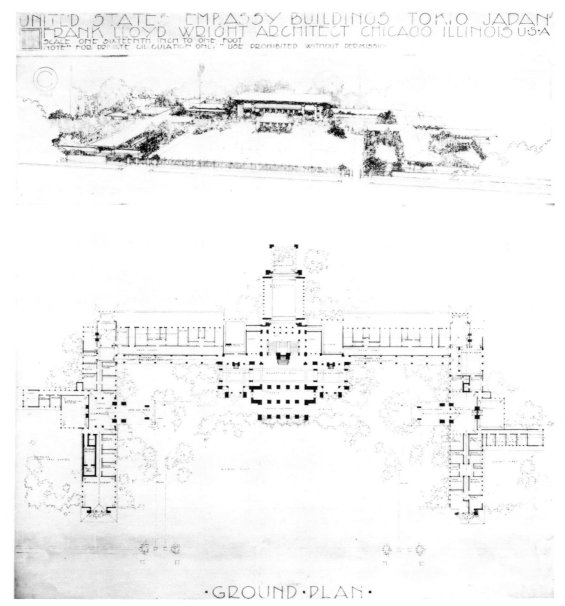

82. Frank Lloyd Wright

Henry J. Allen House, Wichita, Kansas, 1917

Garden   .

Cooper-Hewitt Museum: Smithsonian Regents' Acquisitions Fund and Friends of Drawings and Prints

83. Henry J. Allen House

Furniture views: piano bench and tabouret

Pencil and colored pencils on tracing paper; 37×45.2 cm.

Cooper-Hewitt Museum: Smithsonian Regents' Acquisitions Fund and Friends of Drawings and Prints

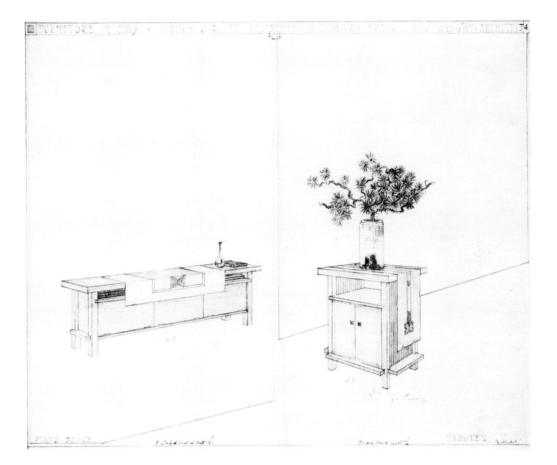

84. **George M. Niedecken for Hermann von Holst; Marion Mahony, designing architect**

David M. Amberg House, Grand Rapids, Michigan, 1910

Living room table, easy chair, and tabouret

Pencil on tracing paper; 19.1 × 30.5 cm.

The Prairie Archives Collection, Milwaukee Art Museum, Gift of Mr. and Mrs. Robert L. Jacobson

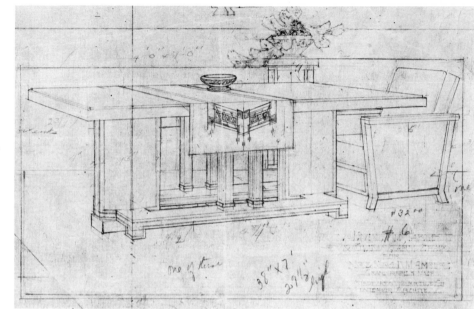

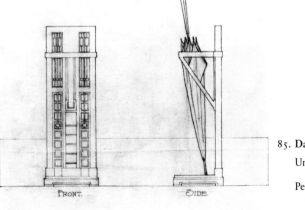

FRONT.   SIDE.

85. **David M. Amberg House**

Umbrella stand, ca. 1911

Pencil on tracing paper; 29.3 × 22.8 cm.

The Prairie Archives Collection, Milwaukee Art Museum, Gift of Mr. and Mrs. Robert L. Jacobson

86. Frank Lloyd Wright

Tazaemon Yamamura House,
 Ashiya, Japan, 1918

Hall table

Keyaki; 75 × 151.2 × 40.7 cm.

H. Solomon

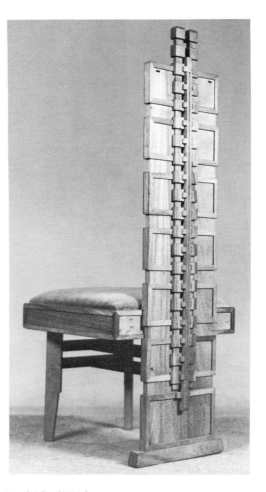

87. Frank Lloyd Wright

Aline Barnsdall "Hollyhock" House

Dining room chair, ca. 1920

Oak, upholstered seat;
 116.2 × 45.1 × 50.8 cm.

City of Los Angeles, Cultural Affairs
 Department, Hollyhock House

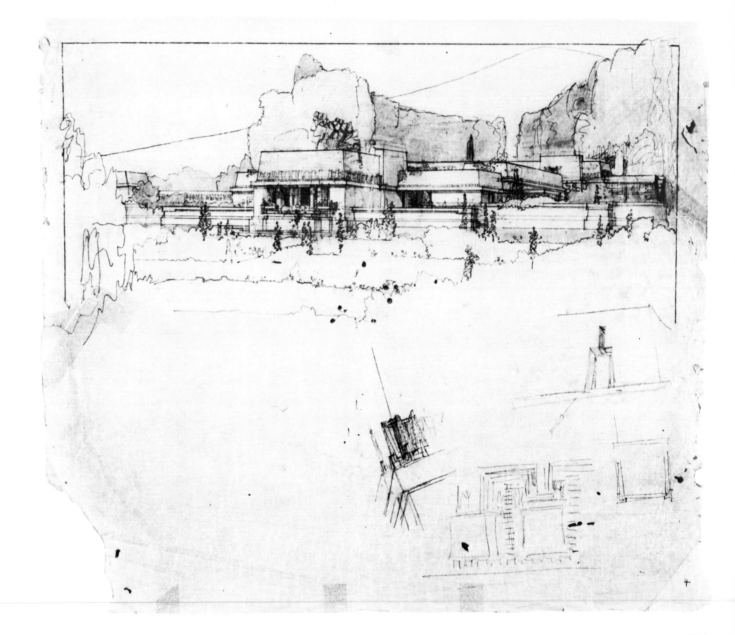

88. **Aline Barnsdall "Hollyhock" House**

Perspective

Pencil and colored pencils on tracing
    paper; 45.7 × 53.4 cm.

City of Los Angeles, Cultural Affairs
    Department, Hollyhock House

89. **Walter Burley Griffin; rendering by
    Marion Mahony Griffin**

Stinson Memorial Library, Anna,
    Illinois, 1913

Perspective and plan

Pen and black ink on linen; 94 × 56
    cm.

Mary and Leigh Block Gallery,
    Northwestern University, Gift of
    Marion Mahony Griffin

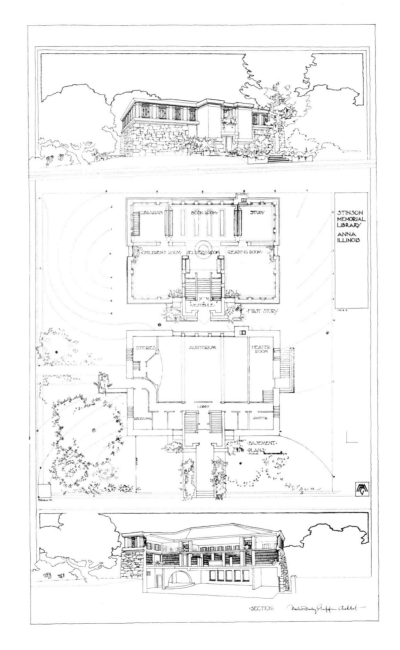

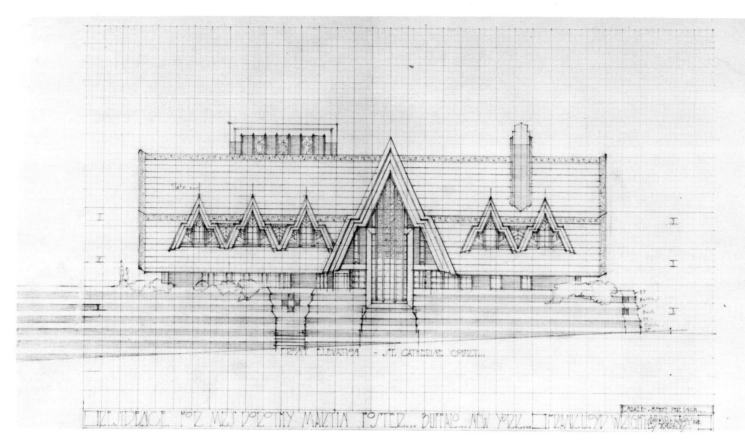

90. Frank Lloyd Wright

Project: Mrs. Dorothy Martin Foster
  House, Buffalo, New York, ca.
  1923

Front elevation

Pencil and colored pencils on paper;
  39 × 54 cm.

Kelmscott Gallery, Chicago, Illinois

91. Frank Lloyd Wright

Project: Fir Tree Cabin, Tahoe Summer Colony, Emerald Bay, Lake Tahoe, California, 1922–23

Perspective

Colored pencils on tissue; 47 × 43.2 cm.

Mr. and Mrs. Michael Pado

Index

Boldface numerals refer to color plates (col. pl.), plates (pl.), and figures (fig.). Buildings are indexed both under their own name (Robie House) and also under that of the architect (Wright: Robie House)